RAVINIA
*The Festival at Its
Half Century*

RAVINIA: THE FESTIVAL

AT ITS HALF CENTURY

Ravinia Festival Association
in conjunction with
Rand McNally & Company

Editor and Project Coordinator: Fannia Weingartner
Research and Captions: Lisa Swanson Weirich
Design and Layout: Harvey Retzloff

Library of Congress Catalog Card Number 84-062426
ISBN: 0-528-81066-9

This book is dedicated to
the generations of performers and audiences
whose enthusiasm and devotion
have made Ravinia what it is today.

ACKNOWLEDGMENTS

The Ravinia Festival Association gratefully acknowledges the guidance, support, assistance, and enthusiastic interest of many people in the preparation of this anniversary book. Through the resourceful efforts of trustees William J. McDonough and David Ofner, co-chairmen of the 50th Anniversary Committee, this special project was undertaken and received their important counsel during the many months of its development. Tom Levine, artist and chief aide to the Festival's music director, was an early and constant contributor of valuable ideas and information for the book. Photographer Robert M. Lightfoot III provided a treasure trove of photographs for this volume. Numerous photographs were supplied by the late photo-journalist Jacqueline Durand, others by B. F. Stein.

Appreciation and deeply felt regard is extended to the authors of the various segments of this history, all of whose lives have been intimately associated with Ravinia: Claudia Cassidy, Edward Gordon, James Levine, and Robert C. Marsh. The contribution of the late Percy B. Eckhart came from our Archives.

Our special thanks go to the co-publisher of this book, Rand McNally & Company, whose team of experts headed by product director Russell L. Voisin, with production editor Rita Stevens serving as liaison, worked closely with Ravinia throughout the development of the book, providing technical knowledge and warm interest.

The Festival's great appreciation is expressed to Charlis McMillan, Ravinia's dedicated manager of communications, for her thoughtful guidance and many contributions. Special thanks also go to Suzanne Thomson of New York for her innumerable, valuable suggestions and contributions; Mrs. Lawrence F. McClure, a Ravinia life trustee; Robert Kular of The Orchestral Association in Chicago; Robert Brubaker, Grant Dean, and the graphics collection staff of the Chicago Historical Society; Robert Robinson of the Highland Park Historical Society; and the reference staffs of The Newberry Library, the Music Library of Northwestern University, the *Chicago Sun-Times*, and the *Chicago Tribune*. Assembling materials for reference was a monumental task at which several research assistants worked tirelessly, especially Jennifer Seaver, Margaret Kulash, Catherine Horan, and Kevin Kelly.

The following graciously gave permission for the use of their illustrations in this book: James Camner, editor of *The Great Opera Stars in Historic Photographs;* Claudia Cassidy; Chicago Historical Society; *Chicago Sun-Times; Chicago Tribune;* Dr. Anna Lou Dehavenon; Edward Gordon; Robert and Marion Marcellus; the Musical Arts Association of Cleveland; Mr. and Mrs. Samuel R. Rosenthal; and the Weicher family of Chicago.

The challenging task of bringing the book to fruition—searching for historical photos, organizing archival material, defining the structure, creating the design, selecting and editing the final components, and coordinating the production details—was accomplished by the talented and dedicated team of principal researcher Lisa Swanson Weirich, designer Harvey Retzloff, proofreaders Carole S. Presser and Meg Walter, and most particularly, editor-in-chief Fannia Weingartner.

CONTENTS

FOREWORD

The fascinating chronicle of Ravinia's origin and development is a cornucopia of beautiful sights and sounds, of enchanting visions remembered and enriching experiences recalled.

Ravinia has been nourished over the decades by the quality of its performances, the artists from around the world who have appeared on its stages, and the unique charm of its environment. Enthusiastic audiences and generous benefactors, in increasing numbers, have fostered the Festival's growth through the years.

This book is a journey through Ravinia's yesterdays to its arrival at half century as an arts festival, with a side trip into the future.

This is not a conventional history, but rather an intimate memoir of Ravinia that captures the moments as they were lived, with one remembrance leading to another. Even the pre-Festival years are recounted by those with a keen recollection of the period and a personal view of the past.

To create a feeling of continuity without the restraints imposed by chronology, Ravinia's long and lustrous life is divided into three eras that sometimes merge in a montage of memories, but their separation in time becomes evident as the story unfolds.

The first patrons to enter Ravinia's gates arrived on August 15, 1904, to enjoy the entertainment offered by an amusement park that boasted a dazzling electric fountain, a baseball field with a grandstand, a merry-go-round, a theater with a pipe organ, a casino for dining and dancing, and soon a concert pavilion.

In the decade that followed, the thirty-six acres of beautiful woodland in Highland Park, Illinois, on Chicago's North Shore, became the setting for symphony concerts, dance, and theatrical performances. By 1914, symphony concerts were alternating with evenings devoted to opera, and from 1919 to 1931, Ravinia was known as the summer opera capital of the world, presenting grand opera in lavish productions with superb casts.

Ravinia took on a new life in 1936 as an international festival of the arts, with concerts by the Chicago Symphony Orchestra as the featured events. In that first festival year, attendance was 52,717 for a six-week summer season, offering twenty orchestral concerts. Today, the Orchestra's concerts during its eight-week residency remain the centerpiece of a three-month calendar of performances by eminent recitalists, chamber musicians, popular entertainers, guest orchestras, ballet and dance companies, and theatrical ensembles. Last season's attendance passed the 425,000 mark, and, as this book goes to press, we expect to signal another record-breaking year in 1985 when we celebrate the Festival's golden jubilee.

A special anniversary offers an irresistible opportunity to pass on what one knows, to share sig-

nificant moments, and recapture parts of life so worth remembering. When I joined the Festival in 1968 I spent considerable time becoming familiar with Ravinia's history before mapping plans for the future. I found the rich tradition of the years from 1914 to 1931 compelling, and nothing seemed more fitting than to bring back full evenings of opera to the place where they had been so loved earlier in the century.

On July 31, 1969, Ravinia heard opera performed once again—a concert performance of *Madama Butterfly* with Martina Arroyo in the title role. It is hard to find words to describe the impact of Arroyo's entrance that night. Even before she became visible her glorious voice began to spin out over the house, growing from the distance as she approached the waiting Pinkerton, sung by Franco Tagliavini. Regal in her bearing but delicate in her movements, Martina perfectly evoked the image of the tragic young Japanese bride-to-be, even though she was not in costume. I turned to John Edwards, the general manager of the Chicago Symphony, seated next to me, to ask for his reaction, but he could not answer—his eyes were wet with tears. That is a particularly poignant memory I have of my late colleague.

At that time, there was considerable risk in presenting opera—no one could predict whether a public unaccustomed to opera performances at the Festival would buy a sufficient number of tickets to meet the increased cost of having a cast of soloists and a chorus on stage, in addition to the orchestra. But Ravinia's trustees encouraged such

innovation as part of the Festival's new direction in programming.

The implementation of new, exciting, and challenging goals for Ravinia has been made possible with the support and understanding of a succession of sensitive and knowledgeable trustees. Individually and collectively they have played a remarkable role in the growth of the Festival, bringing to the organization critically needed resources of money, personal and professional expertise, and important influence in the community. And, significantly, they have recognized the importance of allowing the free artistic development of the Festival. They might well serve as role models for trustees in today's arts world.

The process by which the Festival evolved from management by volunteers to management by professional staff has been strongly supported by all the chairmen and their committees during my tenure at Ravinia. In the course of my seventeen years with the Festival, I have worked with five of the total of eleven chairmen who have served during the fifty years of the Festival's history. Each of those five brought a distinctive personality, special qualities of leadership, and individual talents and strengths to the successful operation of the Festival. They continued the outstanding record of stewardship established by the chairmen of earlier days. Remembering their chairmanship years gives me an opportunity to recall some of the major accomplishments of the Festival during those times.

Stanley M. Freehling, the first chairman with whom I worked, gave unstintingly of his widely

James Levine and Edward Gordon make plans in Gordon's office backstage at Ravinia.

Misha Dichter talks about pianos with Edward Gordon before rehearsal.

known abilities in the service of the arts when he launched Ravinia's first capital campaign for the desperately needed rebuilding of the Pavilion's stage and its backstage area. Another of our priorities was the installation of a state-of-the-art sound system for the lawn to bring the full benefit of the performances on stage to that important audience. The system received its first large-scale updating just before the opening of the 1984 season.

The second chairman of my time was Marion Lloyd, whose imagination and willingness to consider change were tremendous assets during a period of artistic growth. She enthusiastically endorsed my request to appoint the then twenty-eight-year-old James Levine to Ravinia's music directorship, which received the full support of the board. Under her leadership a program of community relations was begun to achieve a spirit of mutual understanding and cooperation between Ravinia and its resident neighbors as the Festival attracted larger audiences each season. It has worked well during the past dozen years. In Mrs. Lloyd's term the Association began the Murray Theatre renovation, completed the new restaurant complex, and embarked on a second capital campaign to provide Ravinia with its first endowment fund.

Richard J. Farrell led that campaign "To Assure Ravinia's Future" before succeeding to the chairmanship of the Festival. A man of many accomplishments and interests, he was chairman during the early years of James Levine's tenure as music director, and was totally supportive of adventurous plans in programming, whether for a Mahler Cycle

or opening the season with a performance of Schoenberg's *Gurrelieder.* Facility improvements and construction continued.

By the time Kent Duncan became chairman in 1979, Ravinia's new artistic directions had become clear, firm, and successful in attracting a loyal public. Among forward-looking plans for the Festival during his administration was a "Challenge Campaign" to meet the matching requirements of a challenge grant from the National Endowment for the Arts to increase Ravinia's endowment fund. Duncan also took special interest in the appearance of the park and the maintenance of its facilities, encouraging such improvements as the installation of an underground sprinkler system for the meadow and an automatic switch-over electrical system to enable power throughout the park to be restored within three seconds after a failure.

Donald G. Lubin, chairman since 1981, has had many ambitions for the Festival, serving as the chief proponent of audience development and broadening the base of Ravinia's financial support. Efforts have been extended to spreading knowledge of the Festival abroad and focusing wider attention on Ravinia's illustrious history. During his term the groundwork has been firmly laid for another period of exciting developments that will propel the Festival into its next half century. The most immediate one is the establishment of a performance-oriented Young Artists' Institute. This has long been my hope for the Festival, and Don Lubin has put his energies to work to help bring it about. But more of this later.

11

From the Archives: A 1945 Perspective

BY PERCY B. ECKHART

Ravinia—its story is the story of an era. It has progressed chameleon-like from an amusement center—a device to stimulate business for a railroad—with baseball park, winter sports, a theater, a dance floor, restaurants, and concerts successively displacing each other, until, during the fabulous era of the 1920s, it culminated in the most spectacular summer opera company in the world.

Now Ravinia is back to concerts again. The opera is a thing of memory and every thought of the original amusement center has vanished. The years have created an aura about Ravinia which you cannot escape. A tradition and a nimbus linger there, for its history is rich. Here are its memoirs.

About 1902 the A. C. Frost Company purchased some thirty-six acres south of Lambert Tree Avenue in Ravinia, now part of the City of Highland Park. The railroad tracks bisect these acres, sixteen of which lie east of the railroad and are well wooded. In the autumn of 1903 a number of buildings were constructed in the eastern portion of what is now Ravinia Park, to create a superior type of amusement park with the hope that popular de-

mand would support it and at the same time furnish patronage for the railroad, of which Mr. Frost was president. A baseball diamond with a permanent grandstand was constructed in the northwest corner of the part lying east of the railroad, and a colorful electric fountain [since replaced by a petunia bed] was placed east of the athletic field.

Just inside the main gate a modern theater was built and equipped with a fine pipe organ. To the south of the theater was a refectory building [the Casino] with a number of dining rooms of various sizes and a dance floor. The grounds were carefully landscaped so as to use the attractive native woods to the best advantage. The opening of the park came in the fall of 1904 with a series of plays in the theater, and plans were made to give them throughout the year. It soon became apparent, however, that a public could be attracted only during the summertime, and the next year saw the construction of the open-air Pavilion, with 1,420 seats and an elevated stage, backed by a concave wooden sound board with extraordinary acoustic properties.

Some of the earlier outdoor summer entertainments were held near the electric fountain. There

In addition to the Pavilion (*below*) Ravinia Park boasted an auditorium (now the Murray Theatre) with a pipe organ and seating for more than 1,000.

was barefoot dancing by Ruth St. Denis and Ted Shawn and performances by Joan Sawyer and her partner, who were then pioneers in fine ballroom dancing. The Ben Greet Players presented open-air Shakespearean performances using a rustic stage on a raised terrace outlined with shrubbery. One of the most successful was *A Midsummer Night's Dream*, with an orchestra conducted by Chevalier N. B. Emanuel. A theatrical company organized by Donald Robertson presented a series of Ibsen plays in the indoor theater, and dancing and dinner parties in the refectory building were promoted more or less successfully.

The baseball diamond proved not to be as attractive as expected and little use was ever made of it. One winter, in the large open space on the west side of the tracks, toboggan slides were constructed and an attempt was made to promote winter sports, but little success attended that effort, and both the winter sports and the plays in the theater were discontinued.

Following the receivership of the Chicago & Milwaukee Electric Railroad, A. C. Frost Company, the corporation organized by the president of the railroad to hold title to Ravinia Park, also went into receivership. George W. Seward, receiver for A. C. Frost Company, was anxious to dispose of the park by a quick sale. About 1910 it was apparent that Ravinia was not to be successful financially, and this was made the more certain following a year or two of stormy summer weather.

In the early spring of 1911 the receiver again expressed a desire to dispose of the property with-

out further delay and there was considerable apprehension among residents of the North Shore that someone might purchase the park and convert it into a cheap amusement center or subdivide it for small houses.

Influenced by this fear Frank R. McMullin, who owned a beautiful home in Ravinia, conceived the idea of organizing a group of North Shore citizens to purchase the park and operate it in a manner that would make it an asset to the entire North Shore. Mr. McMullin asked his attorney, Percy B. Eckhart, to organize a corporation to be known as The Ravinia Company. Mr. McMullin and his friends sold $55,000 worth of stock to many North Shore residents, and then, for $105,000, purchased

The A. C. Frost Company's Chicago & Milwaukee Electric Railroad carried the first patrons to the company's amusement park at Ravinia in 1904.

Walter Damrosch rehearses the New York Symphony at Ravinia. Hailed as "the great society event of the season," the Damrosch engagements between 1905 and 1910 brought afternoon and evening concerts every day for six weeks. The 1910 program (*above*) included a Request Night during which, it was announced, "Mr. Damrosch will be governed in his choice of selections by the requests received."

from the receiver the title to the thirty-six acres known as Ravinia Park, placing a $50,000 first mortgage on the land. (This was paid off in May 1942.)

The new Ravinia Company, having saved Ravinia from the fate of becoming a cheap amusement center or an undesirable real estate venture, now brought good music to the North Shore. Frederick Stock gave some concerts with the Chicago Symphony Orchestra, and Chevalier Emanuel again conducted the Philharmonic Concert Orchestra [probably a local pick-up orchestra] at Ravinia. The Minneapolis Symphony played under Emil Oberhoffer and a Russian orchestra under the direction of Modest Altschuler performed.

Beginning in 1912 the orchestral concerts were combined with one act from some of the popular grand operas. Louis Eckstein, a vice president of The Ravinia Company, developed the idea of giving more importance to the operatic portion of the program, and beginning in 1913 one or two acts from an opera were given nearly every evening of the week. During a long intermission after the orchestral numbers, the audience adjourned to the theater to see moving pictures or to dine and dance in the open-air refectory [probably a remodeling of the old carousel structure] which had just been constructed where it now stands. In 1914 whole evenings were devoted to opera, and although most of the standard operas were shortened by the omission of one act, Ravinia became known throughout the country for masterly presentation of an intimate sort of grand opera with superb casts.

For the thirteen years from 1919 through 1931, under Mr. Eckstein's lavish hand, the golden period of opera brought the greatest singers in the world to Ravinia Park and it became known everywhere as the summer opera capital. Among Ravinia's first operas was *Cavalleria Rusticana*. In the following year were heard scenes from *Aida, Lohengrin, Martha, Carmen, Faust, I Pagliacci, Il Trovatore, Thaïs, Lucia di Lammermoor, Rigoletto,* and *The Tales of Hoffmann*. Soon the repertoire included *Tosca, La Bohème,* and *Madama Butterfly*.

Among the great singers engaged were Lucrezia Bori, Claire Dux, Elisabeth Rethberg, Florence Easton, Edith Mason, Claudia Muzio, Rosa Raisa, Giovanni Martinelli, Edward Johnson, Virgilio Lazzari, Giacomo Rimini, Léon Rothier, Charles Hackett, Mario Chamlee, Tito Schipa, José Mojica, Armand Tokatyan, Antonio Scotti, Ina Bourskaya, Gladys Swarthout, and Louis d'Angelo.

The conductors most often directing were Gennaro Papi, Richard Hageman, and Louis Hasselmans. New and seldom-sung operas given successfully included Auber's *Fra Diavolo*, Falla's *La Vida Breve*, Giordano's *Fedora*, Leoncavallo's *Zaza*, Rabaud's *Mârouf*, Deems Taylor's *Peter Ibbetson*, Ravel's *L'Heure Espagnole*, Puccini's *La Rondine*, Massenet's *La Navarraise*, and Mascagni's *L'Amico Fritz*. Ravinia supported a chorus of some forty voices, selected from both the Chicago and Metropolitan opera companies, an orchestra of fifty men from the Chicago metropolitan opera companies [*sic*] and an orchestra of fifty men from the Chicago Symphony Orchestra. The scenery

Among the park's early attractions was "high-class vaudeville…(with) some of the foremost entertainers of European and American stage." They included "The Girl with the Auburn Hair," "Powell's Marionettes," and "Eight Bedouin Arabs." Later there would be Hungarian fortune tellers, as this photo shows.

A group of Ravinia supporters photographed in 1917.

After the A. C. Frost Company went into receivership, a group of North Shore residents formed The Ravinia Company to purchase the park and preserve it as a place for music making. This $100 share in the company is dated July 1911.

19

Kirsten Flagstad appeared at Ravinia in the summer of 1940 singing principally Grieg and Wagner. As were many artists, she was caught in America by the outbreak of World War II in Europe.

Mrs. Louis Eckstein, who deeded Ravinia Park (part of her husband's estate) to the Festival Association, having lunch with Percy B. Eckhart in 1949.

of an inch deep in this rock, will not soon be obliterated. Time alone cannot remove it.

The Festival Association's offering of music to the public is always given at less than actual cost. In the last nine years the deficit, which averages between $12,000 and $15,000, has been paid by a growing group of guarantors. These generous supporters of Ravinia have steadily increased until they now number about 450, and the amount subscribed has grown progressively throughout successive seasons.

The attendance at the concerts has shown a steady and gratifying increase. Last year the total attendance for the season was over 94,000, an average of 3,920 for each of the concerts. On special occasions, with popular soloists, the attendance at the park has been tremendously increased. The largest audience so far heard Arthur Rubinstein, the great pianist, in 1943—a total of 8,423 persons. In 1936 George Gershwin, appearing in an all-Gershwin program, had 7,831 persons in the audience. In 1944 Alexander Brailowsky brought out 7,686. In 1940 Kirsten Flagstad drew the fourth largest audience of 7,593. Yehudi Menuhin in 1941 had an audience of 7,505.

During the last five years Ravinia has had a final week devoted to chamber music by either the Budapest String Quartet or the Pro Arte Quartet. These intimate chamber music concerts have brought out remarkably large audiences. In August 1941, 2,853 people attended. At that time Benny Goodman played the clarinet [with the Budapest], augmenting it to a quintet.

It is the purpose of the Festival Association to present only the very best of music, and, while the classics have been drawn on mostly, nevertheless modern, living composers have had their best works presented by Ravinia. Over 175 different composers' works have been presented during the previous nine seasons. Wagner has been performed 91 times, Beethoven 71 times, Tchaikovsky 51 times, Brahms 47 times, Richard Strauss 36 times. Among the modern composers, Ravinia has given works by Samuel Barber, Leonard Bernstein, John Alden Carpenter, Aaron Copland, Roy Harris, Paul Hindemith, Serge Prokofieff, William Schuman, Dimitri Shostakovich, Deems Taylor, and David Van Vactor.

Ravinia is operated by a corporation not for profit, managed by trustees and officers who serve without compensation and undertake to manage the park and the affairs of the Association in a businesslike manner. In each of the last five years sixty percent of the contributions made by pre-season guarantors have been returned to them at the end of the season.

Improvements and enlargements of the park, designed to add to the comfort and pleasure of patrons, are being gradually made as material and labor become available.

The Festival Association has two purposes in mind. One is to present music of the highest standards for less than cost, and the other is to assure, by every means possible, the permanence and growth of Ravinia as an educational institution devoted to fine music.

Ravinia: A Charmed Life Then and Now

BY CLAUDIA CASSIDY

Some men have a yacht, I have Ravinia." That was Louis Eckstein, the Chicago businessman with a passion for opera who was the founder and for twenty years the impresario and major Maecenas of the bewitched little opera house in the flowering park about twenty-five miles up Chicago's North Shore. Ravinia today is more the size of an oceanliner. Surely it would fascinate Louis Eckstein that while the Chicago Symphony Orchestra long ago moved from the pit to the stage, Ravinia's skipper in the sense of music director is James Levine, who holds the same post at the Metropolitan, who has been known to open seasons with concert versions of opera, and who introduced Jessye Norman as Isolde summers before she made her Metropolitan debut in the centennial season opening with *Les Troyens*. It would have been interesting too to hear Otto Kahn on all this. The Metropolitan mogul often came to Ravinia openings and he said of its Chicago and Metropolitan opera stars, "They sing better here than they can sing." He also said that Ravinia had the best audience. Flattery aside, surely the most pampered.

How to tell anyone who was not there what it was like? The resonant little Pavilion seating about 1,400, Japanese lanterns swaying in the breeze, the cream of two great opera houses—stars, comprimarios, and chorus—fifty members of the Chicago Symphony Orchestra with first desk men, Gennaro Papi and Louis Hasselmans to conduct. A wide range of thirty-odd operas every night for ten weeks, with concerts on Sunday afternoons. As for a closing Labor Day gala, how about Lucrezia Bori and Tito Schipa in the second act of *Manon*, Rosa Raisa and Giovanni Martinelli in the first act of *Butterfly* (*that* was a duet), and Bori and Martinelli in the passionate third act of *Manon Lescaut?* You don't believe it? I thought not.

How could this happen? Well, once upon a time before what Bori called "the suppression," Chicago had two of the great opera lures of the world, and their twenty-year span was almost identical. Resident opera struck spectacular root at the Auditorium in 1910–11 when in a dazzle of stars Mary Garden sang Mélisande, Louise, Thaïs, Marguerite, and Salome. Percy Hammond called Salome "a fabulous she-thing," and self-appointed moni-

tors of morals called the opera other things. *Salome* was withdrawn until 1921–22 when Garden was that fabulous and expensive item she called "directa."

To read about those seasons is to lament not being there. To help them continue forever Samuel Insull built the Civic Opera House whose office rental was to support opera in splendor—in fact, in the style to which it had been accustomed. The new theater opened November 4, 1929, with a sumptuous *Aida*, and with the stock market crash still quivering. Opera's splendor shuddered and survived through the season of 1931–32, then faded. There were brave and sometimes distinguished efforts after that, and there were seven years of silence until Lyric spiraled into the stratosphere in 1954.

If our first resident opera was Versailles, while it lasted, Ravinia Opera in its bosky intimacy was the Petit Trianon. Except that it was not a plaything. Ravinia Opera was the real thing in high style, with a special flair for the intimate, the instinctively elegant, and on certain nights the indelibly combustible.

The special luxury was the rapport. The little stage with its blue velvet curtains cajoled and cherished the warmest, richest, most sharing sound. The evening often started with smiles, because when Papi was in the pit his shadow cast a spidery web on the ceiling, and he always pulled his nose just before he began. On the combustible closing night Martinelli came to the press room to say goodbye. He had not yet quite returned to earth, nor had any of us (remember that after singing

Isolde, Kirsten Flagstad used to drink champagne to get back down).

If I say that in those days a choice seat cost about $3.50, and that Louis Eckstein told me that the music cost about $65,000 a week—not counting upkeep of the park and the downtown offices—I will be picketed as unfair to impresarios. Ten weeks added up to $650,000, a lot of money then, even for priceless opera—today it would have Ravinia's managers dancing the Highland Park fling.

How did it begin? Louis Eckstein was on the scene when a group from Chicago and the North Shore took over what had been a railroad's amusement park. There were concerts conducted by Frederick Stock. There were dancers, one of them Ruth St. Denis. The Ben Greet Players came on a night so chill that rumor insisted the only warm person in the place was Puck on a dead run through *A Midsummer Night's Dream.*

The original wooden Pavilion, designed by architect Peter J. Weber, served Ravinia audiences from 1905 until 1949. This photo was taken on opening night, June 26, 1926.

RAVINIA
SEASON 1918

Louis Eckstein, a Chicago businessman, became a leading figure in The Ravinia Company, which purchased Ravinia Park from the defunct A. C. Frost Company in 1911. He remained deeply involved with Ravinia until the Great Depression closed it down in 1931.

Program covers from the opera years (*right and on page 24*) were elegantly designed.

Picture Section

Chicago Sunday Tribune.
THE WORLD'S GREATEST NEWSPAPER

August 14, 1927

GIOVANNI MARTINELLI looks here like an aristocrat of the eighteenth century taking a placid stroll in the ancestral park. You will find him looking exactly this way in some of his roles on the Ravinia stage, plus the famous tenor voice that does not appear in the picture.

FLORENCE MACBETH, American soprano, a native of Minnesota, if you insist upon exactness, has been one of the Ravinia stars for a series of seasons. This year she is back in her accustomed position, and the critics say that she is singing better than ever.

ELISABETH RETHBERG permits a view of how Marguerite looked the day she was walking home and met Faust in the market place. Later in the course of the opera she had occasion to look more sorrowful, but this picture is not concerned with tearful endings.

GIUSEPPE DANISE is about to tell how a professional humorist feels in the hours when he is off duty and can take the time to consider his own private and personal affairs. Specifically, he is Rigoletto in the opera of the same name, a part in which he is famous at Ravinia. (Color photos by Godfrey Lundberg.)

INA BOURSKAYA is a singing actress of the mezzo-soprano persuasion, both tragedian and comedian, and blessed with the gift of tongues. She sings Italian and French, speaks English fluently, and would be willing to sing Russian and Polish if the Ravinia repertoire permitted.

EDWARD JOHNSON is his real name and the one he uses at the Metropolitan and Ravinia; Edoardo di Giovanni when he used to sing in Italy. Under either name he is a living rebuke to the argument that Americans never get a chance to become prominent in opera.

Edith Mason, whose operatic career spanned some thirty years, was one of Chicago Civic Opera's leading singers and appeared frequently at Ravinia.

Left: Many of the artists of Ravinia Opera's resident company featured on this page of the *Tribune* returned repeatedly during more than a decade of opera productions.

Lucrezia Bori was a favorite artist both of the Metropolitan Opera and of Ravinia Opera. She is shown here as Mary in Deems Taylor's *Peter Ibbetson,* a role she created in New York and sang again at Ravinia.

In 1923 Tito Schipa made his Ravinia Opera debut as the Chevalier des Grieux in Massenet's *Manon,* also singing Romeo in Gounod's *Romeo and Juliet* and Nemorino in Donizetti's *L'Elisir d'Amore.*

The 1931 season of Ravinia Opera was its last. Four seasons passed before music was heard again at Ravinia.

George Gershwin practices in his Highland Park hotel suite for his July 25, 1936, appearance at Ravinia. He died the following year.

manage the Met), who minded that Wagner was cut so we could catch our trains? Bori was a stunning Salud in *La Vida Breve*, a mischievous delight in *La Rondine*, where one Prohibition night a startled cast drank real champagne—sent to Bori by an admirer named Al Capone.

Martinelli once soared into *Andrea Chénier*'s "Improvviso" three times because the lights kept going out—an audience boon. Edith Mason once stopped midflight in the "Jewel Song" because a bug had flown into her throat. She took it out, stepped down to the footlights (not very far), said "*Da capo, Maestro*," and they did. Mario Chamlee once sang the pitch of a train whistle. On the other hand, when Bori sang Fiora in *L'Amore dei Tre Re*, as Garden did downtown, both had the great Virgilio Lazzari as the blind king, and both were sumptuously costumed by Erté.

Truly, Ravinia was a magical place, with Louis Eckstein welcoming us all as he stood beside the fragrant bed of Rosy Morn' petunias—dark jacket, white trousers, straw boater, gold-headed cane, and sometimes a gift of his other love, Sweetheart roses.

No one knew—except possibly Louis Eckstein whose losses had mounted high—that the summer of 1931 would be the end. Ravinia went out on a high but tender note, not untypical of a theater both admired and loved. It reversed the Metropolitan failure of Deems Taylor's *Peter Ibbetson*, based on George Du Maurier's drama of "dreaming true," which Constance Collier had played with John and Lionel Barrymore, while Ethel Barrymore watched from a box. Bori, Johnson, and Lawrence Tibbett were in the Metropolitan cast, Tullio Serafin conducting. Perhaps it was too slight for the big house. But with Bori and Johnson at intimate Ravinia it set off cheers, damp handkerchiefs, and six sold-out performances. Deems Taylor was cheered when he entered, lustily saluted at the end. It was, tears and all, a radiant period.

Louis Eckstein planned to reopen Ravinia, but his death put a period to that, though his generous will stipulated that it was never to be cheapened. Mary Garden slipped away from Chicago opera after a performance of *Le Jongleur de Notre Dame*. Bori retired from singing. It was the end of an era perhaps unique in the history of opera.

Those were difficult times, too, for the Chicago Symphony Orchestra. At the end of the 1934–35 season Frederick Stock told his Orchestra Hall audience that the Orchestra needed more work to survive. That June the Orchestra opened the free concerts in Grant Park, aided by James C. Petrillo, head of the musicians' union, the man who made the trains stop when Jascha Heifetz played. Other heads and bankrolls got together and on July 3, 1936, the Ravinia Festival with the Chicago Symphony Orchestra began.

Ernest Ansermet was the first guest conductor, Willoughby G. Walling the first chairman. A vivid guest was George Gershwin, who brought Bill Daley as conductor for *Rhapsody in Blue* and the Concerto in F. Gershwin wrote, "A more delightful spot for a concert I can not imagine." Many of us were at Ravinia the next summer when the telegraph chattered that George Gershwin was dead at thirty-eight.

But Ravinia had begun a new life. It was a rich time for ripe talent and just about everyone came except Arturo Toscanini and Vladimir Horowitz (nervous about "outdoor" concerts) and Serge Koussevitzky, busy at Tanglewood. Frederick Stock came briefly—he felt the summer field belonged to guests. Artur Rodzinski, Fritz Reiner, Jean Martinon, and Georg Solti came to Ravinia before they took over downtown. Hans Lange and Tauno Hannikainen went on to Orchestra Hall as associate conductors. Ravinia lured Eugene Ormandy, George Szell, Sir Thomas Beecham, Dimitri Mitropoulos, the *wunderkind* Leonard Bernstein, and that Ravinia favorite Pierre Monteux, who told you the difference between an excited conductor and one who made music exciting.

The little Pavilion was an intimate revelation for soloists. Kirsten Flagstad and Helen Traubel sang Wagner; Heifetz, Rubinstein, and Piatigorsky came separately, and later in that trio to end all trios. (Gossips said of that trio that Rubinstein got first billing, Heifetz got the most money, and Piatigorsky got to play solo.) Artur Schnabel came, and Josef Hofmann, Rudolf Serkin and Emanuel Feuermann, Nathan Milstein and Isaac Stern, Dorothy Maynor, Yehudi Menuhin, the young Leon Fleisher. William Kapell came in that brief, blazing trajectory to a heart-storming Rachmaninoff Third. The renowned Budapest Quartet set off a history of chamber music. Benny Goodman came with Teddy Wilson, Lionel Hampton, and the young man with a horn, Harry James. The New York City Ballet, Ballet Theatre, and the Joffrey blazed the dance trail. The Murray was restored for chamber music, theater, and the smaller dance groups from Martha Graham's and Merce Cunningham's to the Hubbard Street Dance Company.

You will note here the shift to the new Pavilion, the only one many a Ravinia fan knows. On a May night in 1949 the little Pavilion burned to the ground. Six weeks later, by a monumental effort, the fourteenth Festival opened on schedule with Fritz Busch the conductor. Everything was ready but the roof, so in came a thirty-three-ton canvas cover meant for B-29 bombers. It was no bomb—in fact, its acoustical charms are wistfully remembered. But the real roof went on and over the seasons stage and sound have been steadily improved in the airy Pavilion seating 3,500, with extra seats at the sides and thirty-six acres of hospitable park for those who drift in with sumptuous picnic baskets. There were 16,000 on hand the summer of 1983 when Luciano Pavarotti sang a truly beneficial benefit for Ravinia and the Lyric Opera.

To christen the new Pavilion Lotte Lehmann sang. So did Joan Sutherland. When the luminous Elisabeth Schwarzkopf walked on stage an awed male voice inquired "She sings, too?" Many a great one came, and many a favorite returned. Igor Stravinsky conducted his own music. Pablo Casals came with his Catalan Nativity *El Pessebre*. Otto Klemperer came, and Eduard van Beinum and Aaron Copland.

These are but glimpses. As the Festival grew Edward Gordon came in as general manager. Seiji Ozawa was for a time music director, István Kertész

The "Million Dollar Trio" became the media's catchy name for the combination of Jascha Heifetz, Arthur Rubinstein, and Gregor Piatigorsky, shown rehearsing in the home of Ravinia trustee Francis Knight for their 1949 Festival concerts. Ravinia audiences, attending the trio's four recitals that season in record numbers, were among the few ever to hear this alliance of three legendary artists in live performance.

35

Music critic Claudia Cassidy at her desk at the *Tribune*.

William Kapell (*below*) returned to Ravinia for six seasons between his 1943 debut and his tragic death in an airplane crash in 1953. Among his Ravinia appearances was a week of chamber music concerts with the Budapest Quartet. He is shown (*below right*) rehearsing at Ravinia with William Steinberg conducting.

Frederick Stock, who served as conductor of the Chicago Symphony Orchestra from 1904 to 1942, led his orchestra at Ravinia on two occasions, in 1937 and 1941.

Artur Rodzinski cancelled his 1938 European tour and instead opened Ravinia's third season in his CSO debut. He was already well known to NBC Symphony radio broadcast audiences.

was principal conductor. In 1971 James Levine stepped in as substitute conductor in Mahler's *Resurrection* Symphony. Mr. Levine was too young to be resurrected, but not to be recognized. In 1973 he returned as music director, a post he still holds. He is music director of the Metropolitan, soon to be artistic director, and he is a regular at Salzburg and Bayreuth. He is conductor, pianist, devoted accompanist, a busy man who never seems flurried. It has been noted that if at Ravinia a streak goes by in a high wind, it is probably James Levine.

When Levine takes off for European festivals, great care is taken about guests, though it is no news to music that great conductors are in short supply. Kurt Masur of the Leipzig Gewandhaus was a bonanza, a big man in the big style. Maxim Shostakovich had his major success with his father's Fifth Symphony, holding up the score in triumph. Younger conductors attracting attention include Simon Rattle, James Conlon, Michael Tilson Thomas, Edo de Waart, Jesús López-Cobos. Visiting orchestras have included the New York Philharmonic, the Cleveland Orchestra, and The Saint Paul Chamber Orchestra led by Pinchas Zukerman, whose 1983 guests included Isaac Stern and Emanuel Ax.

Ravinia is a kind of pianist's paradise. It owns two Steinways, a Bösendorfer, and both its music director and its general manager are pianists. [Baldwin is the official piano of the Festival.] It lures virtuosi from Alicia de Larrocha and Emanuel Ax to Alexis Weissenberg, with André Watts, Horacio Gutiérrez, Garrick Ohlsson, Misha Dichter, the young Ken Noda, and more. Shlomo Mintz is one of its ardent young violinists, while Henryk Szeryng returned for the Beethoven Concerto pure and undefiled. Mstislav Rostropovich gave us his heart's blood in the Dvořák Cello Concerto, while Levine and the Orchestra furnished instant transfusion. The Murray had the Beaux Arts Trio and the exquisite Victoria de los Angeles in rare Spanish songs, with aftermath of flamenco guitar.

Now within sight of its golden jubilee, Ravinia has grown slowly and carefully. Under the sheltering trees it has flowers and sculpture, restaurants in wide variety, an affectionate habit of honoring friends with a tree that grows in Ravinia. Note the glistening newcomer celebrating James Levine's first ten years as music director. Note the Viennese nights, the stellar nights on the popular front stemming from roots struck by Duke Ellington, Ella Fitzgerald, Joan Baez, and more. Note that while a glittering starry night is wonderful for box office and your best bib and tucker, Ravinia can have special charms on nights of rain-enveloping mist.

On such a night Itzhak Perlman sat up there, cracked corny jokes, and played a celestial violin. On such a night Alfred Brendel played with his heart on a most unaccustomed place—on his sleeve—including a magical revelation of Liszt's *Saint Francis of Assisi Preaching to the Birds*.

Meanwhile, how about James Levine? Plainly a big talent on the march. But what I find especially reassuring is that Ravinia trend toward intimacy. He seems to be a sharer, which is less common among conductors than it once was. He likes soloists, and not just at the Metropolitan where it would be hard to get along without them. True, in the Murray Theatre he played four-hand piano with Brendel, their coats off because cuff buttons kept tangling. In that same Murray he was a true accompanist when John Cheek sang *Die Winterreise* and when Håkan Hagegård sang *Dichterliebe*. In the Pavilion he displayed Marilyn Horne and Kathleen Battle, and he and the Orchestra met Rostropovich and Dvořák on the highest ground, where you see the music whole. And there was that night of dense fog when in Haydn's *Lord Nelson* Mass you all but saw the Admiral in the sea fog of quarterdeck, the London fog of Trafalgar Square. As Guthrie McClintic wrote in his notebook when he first saw Katharine Cornell—"Interesting. Watch."

Ravinia-watching in 1984 meant a twelve-week season of wide range and benign weather—weather is benign at Ravinia when it does not rain—a season opening early with the Midwest debut of the Hamburg Ballet, then the focal eight weeks of the Chicago Symphony Orchestra launched by James Levine with Mahler's *Symphony of a Thousand*. A season of special homage to Shakespeare and Mendelssohn (who met in *A Midsummer Night's Dream*), a centerpiece Beethoven triptych with the admired Kurt Masur of the Leipzig Gewandhaus, a whole younger generation of conductors and soloists, often doubling from the Murray into the Pavilion with scarcely time to change a jacket. The San Francisco Ballet returned with its co-director Michael Smuin, who had a blithe salute to the Beatles and, with Francis Ford Coppola, a mes-

Duke Ellington in a photo taken at his last Ravinia appearance in 1971. Ellington's first Ravinia engagement was in 1957, and he returned with his band four more times before his death in 1974.

Kurt Masur conducts a 1984 rehearsal at Ravinia with Dmitry Sitkovetsky as soloist. Masur conducted the Chicago Symphony for the first time in his 1981 debut at Ravinia.

Mstislav Rostropovich made three separate debuts at Ravinia in 1975: as conductor, as cello soloist, and as piano accompanist to his wife, soprano Galina Vishnevskaya.

The Festival at Its Half Century

BY ROBERT C. MARSH

The first downbeat of the new Ravinia Festival came from a giant in European music, Ernest Ansermet, who on July 3, 1936, led the Chicago Symphony in Wagner's prelude to *Die Meistersinger* and the Beethoven Seventh Symphony, followed by Berlioz's *Roman Carnival* Overture, two Debussy nocturnes, and music from Stravinsky's *Firebird* ballet—an ambitious program. He shared the podium that summer with Hans Lange, with well-known Chicago musicians Rudolph Ganz and Henry Weber, and with another European, Willem van Hoogstraten, then conductor of the summer concerts of the New York Philharmonic.

In 1937 the Festival offered a tribute to Louis Eckstein, who had died in November 1935 and whose vision and support had made possible twenty years of Ravinia Opera festivals from 1912 to 1931. The tribute, in the form of an opera concert with Lucrezia Bori, Armand Tokatyan, and Léon Rothier, directed by Gennaro Papi, recalled those early years. That same summer Ravinia presented Frederick Stock, music director of the Chicago Symphony Orchestra. Among his colleagues, con-

ducting the Chicago Symphony for the first time, was Fritz Reiner, who was to succeed Stock on the Orchestra Hall podium sixteen years later. Ansermet, who clearly had been pleased with his experiences the year before, took advantage of an opportunity to return. (Later the war trapped him in Switzerland.)

The public support for the series as the nation recovered from the Great Depression was a testimonial to the men who had restored Ravinia to the life of the community after four summers of darkness. After it first opened in 1904, Ravinia had quickly become the principal center of cultural activities on the North Shore. Even its temporary loss was a hardship, and the opportunity to reopen the park as a summer home for the Chicago Symphony, extending the season of the Orchestra and bringing it closer to the suburban audience, was a call to action.

It was clear that the social changes produced by the depression required a new financial strategy for the support of the concerts. Although Eckstein had a few friends to assist him in underwriting the opera festival, more than half of the annual subsidy

43

Willoughby G. Walling (1936–1937)

Percy B. Eckhart (1938–1950)

Howell W. Murray (1951–1958)

Julien H. Collins (1959–1961)

Earle Ludgin (1962–1964)

Ronald M. Kimball (1965–1967)

Stanley M. Freehling (1968–1971)

Mrs. Glen A. Lloyd (1972–1975)

Richard J. Farrell (1976–1978)

Kent W. Duncan (1979–1981)

Donald G. Lubin (1982–1985)

The Ravinia Festival Association, incorporated in the State of Illinois on April 22, 1936, has had eleven chairmen in its fifty-year history.

term influence on the Festival and its policies. Each applied his own special skills to a major area of management. Percy B. Eckhart, who had served as legal counsel for the Association's incorporation, served as chairman from 1938 to 1950. (The first chairman named in 1936, Willoughby G. Walling, died before the launching of the third season.) Howell W. Murray, an investment banker, raised funds; Renslow P. Sherer, an industrialist, oversaw property maintenance; and Francis M. Knight, another banker, took on the task of securing artists for the Festival. This group guided the fortunes of Ravinia for two decades, assisted in the early years by an advisory committee that included the manager of the Chicago Symphony. Murray succeeded Eckhart as chairman, serving from 1951 to 1958.

A new pattern of shorter tenures was established in the terms of Julien H. Collins (1959–1961), Earle Ludgin (1962–1964), Ronald M. Kimball (1965–1967), and Stanley M. Freehling (1968–1971). During the same period, the issues of how much and what kind of professional help were needed began to be discussed, until in the late 1960s the Festival hired its first management staff and began to formally reorganize its governing structure. A committee report in 1970 stated:

The Ravinia Festival has been chaired by a series of independent and versatile men who have been willing to carry all the problems of the Festival, make most of the decisions, and, as a result, give tremendous amounts of time to the enterprise. This process appears to be neither economical nor predictable in the future....The Ravinia Festival organization must be redefined in terms of its inevitable growth.

The outcome of those observations was a move toward decentralization of power, the wider use of committees and individual committee members, and the creation of the post of president to support the chairman and share in some leadership responsibilities. Mrs. Glen A. (Marion) Lloyd, a member of the committee preparing the report, became the first president and later served as chairman from 1972 to 1975. She was succeeded by Richard J. Farrell (1976–1978), Kent W. Duncan (1979–1981), and the current chairman Donald G. Lubin, whose term began in 1982.

In 1938 Artur Rodzinski of the Cleveland Orchestra and Eugene Ormandy, principal conductor of the Philadelphia Orchestra, two of the greatest names of the day in American music, made their Ravinia debuts. Rodzinski fell in love with the Orchestra and was to become its conductor in 1947. Indeed, of the conductors who have headed the Chicago Symphony since 1936, four, Reiner, Rodzinski, Georg Solti, and Jean Martinon (in that order) established a reputation at Ravinia before being called to Orchestra Hall. Rafael Kubelik, unknown to Ravinia audiences when he was named music director in 1950, came to Ravinia with great success in 1967. Ravinia also supplied the Orchestra with two of its finest associate conductors: Hans Lange, who conducted during the Festival's opening season in 1936 before assuming his downtown post that fall, and Tauno Hannikainen of Finland, who made his debut in 1946 and became the Number 2 man at Orchestra Hall a year later when Rodzinski became music director.

It was at Ravinia on my birthday, August 5, 1938, that—after years of listening to records and radio—I first heard a live symphonic concert. Ormandy was the conductor and the program was Brahms's *Academic Festival* Overture, the Beethoven Seventh Symphony, *Don Juan* and the *Rosenkavalier* waltzes by Richard Strauss, and the polka and fugue from *Schwanda* by Weinberger. My fate was sealed. Serious music became the center of my life.

Sir Adrian Boult appeared at Ravinia early in the summer of 1939, weeks before enemy U-boats threatened to separate him from his native Britain. (In 1949, with the world at peace, he returned for a memorable reunion with the Orchestra.) Rodzinski and Vladimir Golschmann of the St. Louis Symphony directed the remaining programs. Each conductor had eight concerts in two weeks. Ormandy, Rodzinski, and John Barbirolli (then conductor of the New York Philharmonic) were the principal figures of the first wartime summer in 1940.

The following year Ravinia attracted Sir Thomas Beecham, Pierre Monteux of the San Francisco Symphony (who was to keep coming back for two decades), and George Szell—all illustrious Europeans who were making new careers in this country. Monteux's extraordinary repertory and supreme musicianship soon made him a Ravinia institution. There was seemingly nothing he could not play well—and the Orchestra loved him as much as did the public, which was saying a great deal. Beecham found Ravinia "the only railway

John Barbirolli (who became Sir John in 1949) succeeded Toscanini as conductor of the New York Philharmonic in 1937, remaining there until 1942. At Ravinia in 1940 he conducted seven concerts, including a program with Kirsten Flagstad in her only Festival appearance.

George Szell was born in Budapest, grew up in Vienna, and came to the United States in 1939. His legacy at Ravinia includes not only his appearances in the 1940s and 1950s, but his musical influence as teacher and mentor to the Festival's present music director, James Levine.

The conducting career of Sir Adrian Boult was at its height when he visited Ravinia in 1939 (a year in which he also was a guest conductor at the New York World's Fair) and again in 1949. During the 1930s he trained and conducted the newly formed BBC Symphony Orchestra.

It was a rare summer between 1941 and 1961 that Pierre Monteux did not conduct the CSO at Ravinia. He conducted nearly eighty Festival programs in nineteen seasons. In 1961, at the age of eighty-six, he accepted an appointment as chief conductor of the London Symphony

Orchestra (with a twenty-five-year contract) and remained active until 1964. With Monteux in this 1940s photograph is concertmaster John Weicher.

To John Weicher, superb concertmaster and indispensible "left hand" of conductor, with gratitude and appreciation.
Erich Leinsdorf
July 1945.

Erich Leinsdorf first conducted the Chicago Symphony at Ravinia in 1945 as a young man of thirty-two. He returned in 1976 and 1980.

Leonard Bernstein was an assistant conductor of the New York Philharmonic at the time of his Ravinia debut in July of 1944. Some months earlier, as a short-notice replacement for Bruno Walter with the Philharmonic, he had begun his rapid rise to international celebrity.

During the war years Ravinia's audiences were sprinkled with people in uniform and the programs carried blackout instructions (see page 67).

Bernstein's music was one of soprano Jennie Tourel's specialties. She made her Ravinia debut in 1944 with the composer-conductor and then returned three times in the 1950s in a variety of programs.

50

station with a resident orchestra." This ambience did not suit Sir Thomas, and he did not return, but others were prepared to take the passing trains in stride.

The United States was at war when Ravinia opened for the summer of 1942, but the music, with Rodzinski, Szell, Monteux, Ormandy, and the debut of Dimitri Mitropoulos of the Minneapolis Symphony, was dazzling—precisely what our morale required in years when the world seemed to be at hazard. Among the summer dresses and the tropical suits, uniforms of all the services were now visible. Szell's soloist was one of the most eminent pianists of the century, Artur Schnabel, and he played four concerti in four concerts, the Beethoven No. 4, the Mozart C Minor, the Brahms No. 2, and the Beethoven No. 5. Seated on the stage of the old Pavilion in a straight wooden chair—he disliked piano benches—working with a colleague he remembered from the Berlin State Opera, he reminded us how much of the best of European culture had now been transplanted to America.

A week later Ormandy directed the Brahms Double Concerto with Joseph Szigeti and Gregor Piatigorsky. This was music worthy of any major orchestra at the peak of its winter concerts. On August 22, at the close of the season, Stock appeared at Ravinia for the final time. He conducted the recently completed Seventh Symphony by Shostakovich in a special concert for Russian War Relief. His death, early in the 1942–43 season, ended thirty-seven years of uninterrupted leadership for the Chicago Symphony Orchestra.

In 1943 Szell's soloist for a two-week period was Arthur Rubinstein, who played Tchaikovsky's Piano Concerto No. 1 followed by the Brahms No. 2, the Rachmaninoff No. 2, and the Beethoven No. 4. It was also in 1943 that William Kapell made his Ravinia debut, launching a piano career that was to continue through several summers until his tragic death in an airplane accident ten years later.

In 1944 Mrs. Louis Eckstein, who had held title to Ravinia Park in the nine years since her husband's death, carried out his wishes and deeded the property to the Ravinia Festival Association, to be:

devoted to the presentation of concerts by outstanding symphony orchestras and other musical bodies of high artistic purpose and renown and also dramatic art, all designed to uphold the high standards of artistic and educational values heretofore established.

It was a piece of inspired philanthropy that insured the future of the concerts. The good news was part of Percy B. Eckhart's annual greeting. Eckhart, as his contribution to this volume illustrates, established a tradition of grace and wit in his salutations that has rarely been equaled.

Leonard Bernstein, twenty-six and fresh from his debut with the New York Philharmonic, came to Ravinia that year. Erich Leinsdorf, then music director of the Cleveland Orchestra, joined the Ravinia roster in 1945 as the war came to an end, and 1946 saw the first appearance of William Steinberg. It also began a tradition that flourished briefly—a final concert by invitation only that was mostly fun and games. The "Low Art Quartet" was heard, along with a trumpet concerto by jazzman Harry James. Monteux conducted the first such event which contained parts of the *Toy* Symphony then attributed to Haydn (it is really by Leopold Mozart) and closed with some genuine Haydn, the *Farewell* Symphony, with the musicians blowing out the candles on their music stands as they departed during the final movement.

The finest new talents and great figures of a golden age of European conducting appeared at the Festival, which came fully into its own. A commentator of the time called Ravinia "the Salzburg of inland America," and the comparison was apt.

The music was irresistible. In the summer of 1946 I was supposed to be mastering German irregular verbs in anticipation of a language examination the following autumn, but with Szell, Steinberg, and Monteux at Ravinia it was hopeless. I would go to the park early in the afternoon and pretend to study, but it was music that consumed my attention. I never learned the verb forms, never took the examination, and gave up my fellowship, trusting that my fate was linked with music rather than college teaching.

With the world again at peace, the celebrated maestros had a greater choice of summer work, but it is instructive to note how many returned to Ravinia and how many more made their debuts there. High on that list was Fritz Busch, who first came to Ravinia in 1948 and was back the next year. Reiner was there too during both summers, bringing together the conductors who had been the glory of the Dresden Opera in the early 1920s. They pre-

sented Central European repertory with an unfailing sense of tradition. But neither was afraid to try new things. Busch played the Second Symphony of John Alden Carpenter in 1949, and Reiner offered Robert McBride's *Swing Stuff.* In 1948 Ormandy played music by another Chicagoan, Leo Sowerby, whose *Poem for Viola and Orchestra* had William Primrose as soloist. Ormandy was clearly delighted working at Ravinia; the quality of his concerts and the diversity of his repertory told us that. He was back in 1950, 1953, and 1956. Antal Dorati, then head of the Minneapolis Symphony, was a guest in 1950. Kapell, who had played the Khachaturian Piano Concerto with Ormandy the week before, returned to play the Rachmaninoff No. 2 with him.

The summer of 1951 was dominated by two figures: Mitropoulos, now conductor of the New York Philharmonic, who was both soloist and conductor for the Malipiero Piano Concerto No. 4; and one of the most celebrated Italian conductors of the century, Victor de Sabata. His programs were remarkably far-ranging in style. As a gesture to his hosts he played some American music, Morton Gould's *Spirituals,* and to honor his homeland de Sabata presented Respighi's *The Pines of Rome* with the brass marching across the stage at the close like Roman legions on the Appian Way.

Josef Krips, to whom the Viennese tradition was second nature, first came to the Festival in 1953 and returned with regularity until the late 1960s. Szell kept Ravinia on his calendar until 1952, the year in which he shared the podium with Otto Klemperer, the man who had preceded him in his

In a distinguished international career, Antal Dorati has held many important conducting posts. He became a United States citizen in 1947 and made his CSO debut at Ravinia in 1950.

Conductor Dimitri Mitropoulos devoted much effort to enriching concert repertory performed in America. His first Ravinia concert in 1942 included the six-year-old Shostakovich Fifth Symphony, and in later seasons he also performed as both conductor and soloist in Prokofieff's Piano Concerto No. 3 and Respighi's Toccata for Piano and Orchestra.

Robert C. Marsh in his Master of Arts gown, Northwestern University Commencement, June 19, 1946.

Poor health and professional clashes hindered Otto Klemperer's career in the 1940s, but by 1952, when he made his Ravinia debut, he had become widely recognized as the foremost interpreter of the Austro-German repertory from Haydn to Mahler.

The celebrated Hungarian-born American maestro Eugene Ormandy conducted at Ravinia for seven seasons between 1938 and 1956. He is shown above, and at left with the CSO in the old Pavilion.

Eduard van Beinum based his career in Europe, maintaining a long association with the Amsterdam Concertgebouw. His American debut occurred in 1954 and Ravinia welcomed him the following year.

One of the great singing actresses of our time, Elisabeth Schwarzkopf appeared at Ravinia several seasons between 1955 and 1969. She is shown here around the time of her memorable Viennese Night performances in the late 1960s.

Sir Georg Solti, music director of the Chicago Symphony Orchestra, first conducted that orchestra in 1954, at Ravinia. Recalling that event, he said, "My first visit to America was in 1953 to conduct the opera in San Francisco. My second visit was the following summer, my initial encounter with the CSO. When I arrived for the rehearsals I was struck by the seriousness of the orchestra, how quickly we had some programs in one rehearsal and difficult ones in only two rehearsals; they were incredibly quick. I fell in love with them at Ravinia—the marvel of their response, the great standard of their playing. I think they liked me also— we had a very good rapport."

Maestro Solti returned to play with the Chicago Symphony Orchestra at Orchestra Hall in 1968, and was appointed music director in 1969. Commenting further on Ravinia, Solti added, "You have had a very illustrious list of conductors: George Szell, Fritz Reiner, a truly distinguished list, and I know that since I was at Ravinia you have developed enormously. I know you have rebuilt the Pavilion, improved the acoustics and have become an organization with greatly enlarged public support. Your music director [James Levine] is a very good friend of mine. We have a wonderful cooperation with Ravinia."

first important job as head of the Strassburg Opera. Among the programs during his incredible two weeks at Ravinia, Klemperer conducted two all-Beethoven concerts, one of them including the Ninth Symphony. He returned for a week of memorable concerts in 1953, before going to Europe where his career entered its final triumphal phase.

It was not just conductors who caught your attention. Elisabeth Schwarzkopf, who made her debut in 1955 (with Enrique Jorda), guaranteed her return by announcing that she had not flown the Atlantic just to sing two Puccini arias, and offered us Mozart and a Swiss waltz song as well.

As the 1950s drew to a close, Ravinia continued to attract major talents from the younger—and older—generations. Igor Markevitch was a shooting star from 1956 to 1958. Eduard van Beinum was heard briefly in 1955, and Bernstein returned in 1956 before going to the New York Philharmonic. The important debut, and many sensed it at the time, was in 1954, when Ravinia presented Georg Solti in his first American symphonic programs. He introduced himself to Ravinia with the Mozart *Jupiter* Symphony and the Beethoven *Eroica*. He was back in 1956, 1957 (when he offered Haydn's *The Seasons*), and 1958. He said farewell with another performance of the *Eroica* confident, I suspect, that his Chicago reputation was secure. And it was in the same season that Fritz Reiner appeared at Ravinia for the last time. Within a few weeks Ravinia heard the two conductors whose points of view would shape the Chicago Symphony in the final half of the century.

By the late 1950s it was clear that Ravinia had come a long way from its original purpose. As the Eckhart and Cassidy accounts explain, Ravinia Park had been created in 1904 to further the fortunes of the A. C. Frost Company's Chicago & Milwaukee Electric Railroad. This company developed it as an amusement park and experimented to see which attractions would bring the most business. The lesson, quickly learned, was that serious music was the most appealing alternative offered. The success of the New York Symphony Orchestra led by Walter Damrosch during summers from 1905 to 1910, and concerts by the Chicago and Minneapolis orchestras, gave Ravinia its identity. It was to be the home of a music festival.

When control of Ravinia's future passed to a group of community leaders following the bankruptcy of the A. C. Frost Company in 1908, its character as a music festival was confirmed. In 1916 the railroad was sold to a company headed by Samuel Insull and renamed the Chicago, North Shore & Milwaukee, and by 1919 the trains were able to go to the heart of Chicago's Loop through the North Side elevated structure. Ravinia, about twenty-five miles from the center of the city, could now be reached conveniently from any point along the city's electric railway system.

Although Ravinia Park had been created to further the fortunes of Frost's railway, the situation had now been reversed and the railroad would henceforth serve the interests of those who wanted Ravinia to become a cultural center and were eager to make it accessible to a larger public.

Writing in 1930, critic Edward Moore cited New York's great music patron Otto Kahn as saying, "if Ravinia were picked up from where it is and set down somewhere in Central Europe, people would make pilgrimages from all over the civilized world to visit it." Moore went on to note that,

as a matter of fact, they come near to doing that now. The greater part of the patronage is naturally from Chicago and the north shore, brought there by steam, electricity, automobile, and on foot. But many come from great distances.... Tourists from everywhere, native and foreign, make a visit there, and having made one, make others.

The accessibility of the park by rail fostered the newly organized Ravinia Festival's efforts to attract a regular audience from the greater Chicago area.

In addition to the electrically run elevated excursion trains, Ravinia was served by the scheduled North Shore & Milwaukee Railroad, which had built a siding on the southbound part of the track at the park where a special train would wait until the music ended and the final bows had been made, before whisking its passengers into the city. If you were in Chicago and could not drive, you went to Ravinia on the North Shore, which also brought passengers from the other direction—Waukegan, Kenosha, and even Milwaukee.

The opening years of the 1960s saw two major changes in this pattern which had a direct effect upon the Ravinia public. The first was the completion in 1961 of the expressway system which linked the northern suburbs with Chicago. A drive to Ravinia from the city had always been slow. The

Left: The west gate of the park, along the North Shore & Milwaukee railroad tracks, in 1937. *Below:* Today the majority of concert-goers arrive in cars via the expressway system.

streets were narrow and not designed for high speed travel, and the twenty-five mile journey might take nearly two hours if traffic was severe. With the new roads Ravinia could now be reached by car in about a half-hour from most North Side addresses.

The other change was the demise of the North Shore & Milwaukee. The big electric trains served the concerts through the summer of 1962, but on a bleak, wintry night midway in January 1963 the railway that had been hailed as the nation's fastest interurban slipped into history. It could no longer be operated at a profit.

By the summer of 1963 a new pattern had emerged. The Chicago public at Ravinia now consisted overwhelmingly of people who had cars. But whether the public arrived by car or train—the Chicago and North Western Railway Co. (established in 1864) still maintains service to the park—Ravinia has always needed the full base of support that can only be provided by the metropolitan area in its largest sense, and, indeed, its future would seem to require a regional if not a national—or even international—audience. In 1982 the Festival management began a long-term campaign to extend Ravinia's influence, and public, beyond the Chicago metropolitan area.

As a corporate entity Ravinia has always been entirely separate from The Orchestral Association which produces the concerts of the Chicago Symphony in the remaining nine months of the year. Unlike certain other festivals, the Ravinia Festival has never been a replay of highlights from the previous winter season. (Désiré Defauw, in the summers from 1943 through 1945, was the only music director of the Chicago Symphony to appear annually at Ravinia.) It has always had its own conductors, its own programs.

From the start, Ravinia has offered diversified repertory in a conscious attempt to provide the best music in all styles and idioms. George Gershwin was piano soloist with the Orchestra in the first season, drawing 7,831 people, some of whom took to the trees the better to see him play.

The Festival was only two years old in August 1938 when Benny Goodman, the dominant figure in the popular music of the day, brought his orchestra and the other members of his celebrated trio—Teddy Wilson and Lionel Hampton—for a program that reviewed twenty years of jazz as well as playing the current hits. It provided a potential battleground for the jitterbugs and the ickies (the fashionable term for those who failed to appreciate Goodman's art). Whatever else he may have achieved, Goodman drew enough listeners to balance the books for the summer.

In 1940 a different sort of innovation was offered. As the Orchestra took its leave, the Pro Arte Quartet "from Brussels" arrived to play a cycle of the complete Beethoven string quartets. The response in each case showed the audience's interest in having both popular music of the highest quality and the chamber music of the great masters in the regular schedule. Ravinia acquired a new calendar: six weeks with symphony concerts on Tuesday, Thursday, and Saturday evenings and a Sunday matinee, and a seventh week of chamber music on the same pattern, twenty-eight events in all. This format continued through the summer of 1955.

In 1941 the most celebrated string quartet of the day, the beloved Budapest, closed the Ravinia season. It was back the next summer, and the summer following was joined by Szell in the Mozart K. 493 piano quartet, one of the maestro's few public appearances as a pianist, and a performance later recorded in a Hollywood sound studio. (Szell had just completed two weeks of conducting at Ra-

vinia.) In all, the Budapest was at Ravinia nine times, and although after 1944 its appearances were no longer on an annual basis, it continued to return until practically the end of its career. It made its farewell appearance at the Festival in 1961.

The Pro Arte was back in 1945. It was followed in 1946 by the Gordon Quartet, headed by former Chicago Symphony concertmaster Jacques Gordon, with the Albeneri Trio for contrast. In 1947 the chamber music week was replaced for one summer by Alicia Markova and Anton Dolin with a small ballet company. Dance returned to Ravinia with performances by Ballet Theatre in 1954 and 1955, and in 1956 Ravinia audiences saw some of the last performances of the Ballet Russe de Monte Carlo. In 1960 George Balanchine's New York City Ballet came to Ravinia, beginning an association that continued until 1971.

Chamber music carried on in 1948 with the Budapest, whose performances were to be the last heard in the original wooden Pavilion. The final music played under the old roof was Wolf's *Italian*

Far left: Benny Goodman in Chicago at the time of his 1938 appearance at Ravinia. *Near left*: Mr. Goodman in a reunion concert with Lionel Hampton, Teddy Wilson, Gene Krupa, and bassist Leroy "Slam" Stewart at Ravinia in 1973.

Although the original members of the Budapest Quartet were all Hungarian by birth, the group reached its greatest renown during the 1930s with a second generation of members, all of Russian origin. The ensemble, as it appeared at Ravinia for nine seasons, included violinists Joseph Roisman and Alexander Schneider, cellist Misha Schneider, and violist Boris Kroyt.

Nina Novak, a soloist with the Ballet Russe de Monte Carlo, which gave a week of Ravinia performances in the summer of 1956.

Two generations of the Serkin family have added luster to Ravinia's roster of pianists. Rudolf Serkin made four appearances between 1944 and 1956; his son Peter has performed during seven seasons from 1965 to 1984.

A fire, for which no cause could be determined, swept through the original wooden Pavilion forty-six days before the 1949 season was scheduled to open. Photographers arrived just in time to record the scene of a valiant but futile struggle against the flames.

Serenade. The last conductor on the stage was Monteux. On May 14, 1949, the old Pavilion was destroyed by fire, and the chamber music performances of that season were heard in an unusual setting: a new stage and orchestra shell that had been constructed almost overnight with an improvised roof that had once been a tent hangar for World War II bombers.

Chairman Eckhart, opening that season on June 28, prefaced the arrival of Busch to conduct a Wagner program with new heights of oratory:

This serenely secure covering that floats majestically over your blessed heads weighs, with its equipment, 66,000 pounds. It is one of the few things coming out of Southern California, since gold was discovered there exactly one century ago, that is not as screwy as it looks. It is rainproof, fireproof, mildewproof, and mothproof. It will not fade in the sun or be gone with the wind. It will sustain 30 pounds to the square foot as well as a first and second mortgage. It is tasteless and odorless, and you will get double your money back if you can discover how we got the darling up.

In that setting the "Million Dollar Trio," Jascha Heifetz, Gregor Piatigorsky, and Arthur Rubinstein, offered some extraordinary performances.

The new look in 1950 was the rebuilt Pavilion, an expanded version of which remains the center of activity at the Festival. The first conductor on the stage was Ormandy, who dedicated it with his transcription of the C Minor Passacaglia by Bach. The innovation was recitals, the unforgettable Lotte Lehmann accompanied by Paul Ulanowsky, and solo appearances by pianist Claudio Arrau. The Paganini Quartet, one of the fine ensembles of the

Work began immediately on a new stage and the installation of new seats, but there was too little time to build a roof over the audience area. Undaunted, Ravinia trustees found an unorthodox but ingenious solution.

Under the protection of the hastily erected B-29 bomber tent, German-born conductor Fritz Busch is shown preparing for a Wagner program on opening night in 1949. A renowned opera conductor, Busch also led singers Herta Glaz, Uta Graf, Jerome Hines, and Irene Jessner in two evenings of excerpts from Richard Strauss's *Der Rosenkavalier* and Mozart's *The Magic Flute*, *Così fan Tutte*, and *Don Giovanni*.

Lotte Lehmann, shown at home with her dog Mohrchen.

The New York Pro Musica, founded in 1952 by Noah Greenberg, appeared at Ravinia for five seasons between 1957 and 1964.

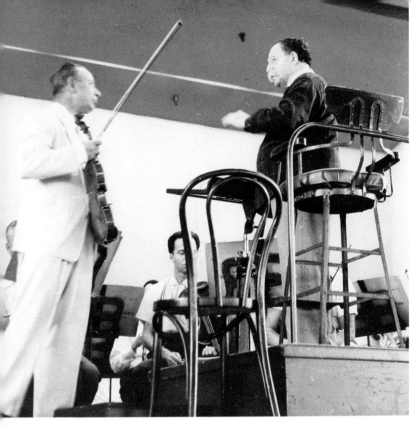

In July of 1956 French violinist Zino Francescatti and conductor Pierre Monteux performed works by Beethoven, Mozart, and Saint-Saëns.

Claudio Arrau at the time of his 1970 recital of Beethoven sonatas to benefit Ravinia's capital campaign. The renowned Chilean pianist first performed at Ravinia in 1948.

Isaac Stern was just twenty-eight but already a veteran of American stages when he made his Ravinia debut in 1948, and his European debut the same year.

day, was present as well. After two more summers with the Budapest, Ravinia engaged a younger group, the Hungarian Quartet, in 1953, and in 1954 went to Chicago's resident quartet, the Fine Arts, which returned in 1960.

Chamber music by celebrated soloists retained its attraction. In 1955 it was provided by the trio of Isaac Stern, Leonard Rose, and Eugene Istomin. They yielded in 1956 to the Griller Quartet. That year also the Beaux Arts Trio, still a Ravinia attraction in the 1980s, made its debut. It came back in 1957, along with the New York Woodwind Quintet and Noah Greenberg's New York Pro Musica, which gave the Ravinia public its first introduction to pre-Baroque and Baroque music. The return of the Budapest in mid-season 1958 reminded us that the role of chamber music had now changed significantly. It no longer stood apart in the final week of the season but was assuming its present role as an integrated part of the Festival throughout the summer. The Budapest took us through familiar repertory from Haydn to Debussy, works it had taught us to love through performances unsurpassed in their warmth and eloquence.

The old Ravinia did not have a full-time manager but was run informally by a small committee of the trustees making the administrative decisions. By the mid-1950s the Festival was facing some financial hardship. In 1956, for the first time in the twenty years since the Guaranty Fund had been established, the Festival was unable to return the traditional refund to guarantors. Some thought

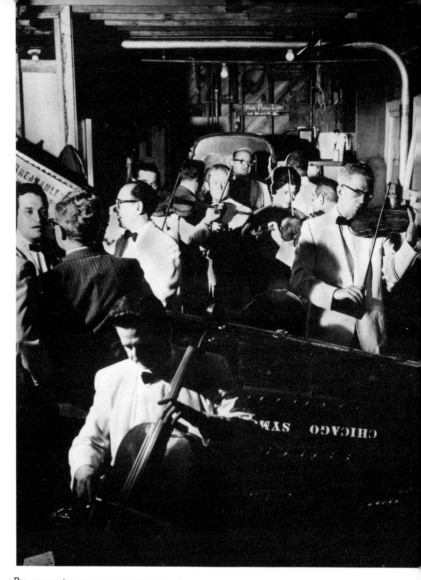

that part of the problem lay in competition from other summer entertainments, especially theater. Others feared that Ravinia was offering too many of the same faces—famous though they might be—playing the same repertory from season to season.

In 1957 every effort was made to freshen the schedule and draw crowds. The Royal Danish Ballet was engaged for a week. The theater (long used as a warehouse) was reopened after forty-two years of darkness with a production of Sean O'Casey's *Pictures in the Hallway*. (However, the theater's potential could not be realized until an air-cooling system was installed in 1963, at which time it was renamed for former chairman Howell W. Murray.) There was a poetry reading by Archibald MacLeish; Cornelia Otis Skinner did her one-woman show; the old Casino housed an art exhibit; there was even a mini-festival of four classic films. Last was a unique entertainment, a series of tableaux entitled *Galerie Vivant* (famous paintings brought to life) by Helen Tieken Geraghty.

The failing attendance was read as a sign of flagging enthusiasm. With increasing frequency the musical community and the critics of the four Chicago newspapers expressed dissatisfaction with the unimaginative programming and the predictable pattern into which the Festival had settled. Even when major artists were engaged, their services were not always used for appropriate repertory. All this seemed to come into focus August 9, 1958, when Edouard Van Remoortel and Josef Fuchs were featured with the Orchestra. Fuchs, a re-

Pre-concert warm-up was accomplished in close quarters before the 1969–70 capital campaign raised funds to build a new backstage area.

A sign erected along the Chicago and North Western tracks in 1951 reminds train engineers to refrain from blowing the whistle as they pass the Festival grounds.

66

In the past, as in the present, the beauty of the park has inspired some patrons to spend pre-concert hours with canvas and paint; others have relaxed with a casual stroll through the grounds and a leisurely snack.

BLACKOUT SIGNALS

✳

The Management of Ravinia Park requests the voluntary cooperation of its patrons in complying with the instructions and recommendations made by the Chief Air Raid Warden's Office of Highland Park to insure their greatest safety in case of a test blackout or an actual raid.

In case of a test blackout or actual air raid there will be intermittent blasts of a siren for an interval. The "all clear" will be noted by a continuous long blast by the siren.

DURING BLACKOUT

✳

Remain where you are at the time the siren sounds. If seated, please remain in your seat. If in the open, sit on the ground. If in your car, stop the car, extinguish lights and remain there.

Please refrain from smoking or striking a light. Any special announcements will be made over the amplifying system.

Should there be an actual raid, remain where you are and be calm. Ravinia Park is some distance from any possible enemy objective and you are comparatively safe.

Ravinia Park attendants have been appointed as Air Wardens. Together with members of the Highland Park Auxiliary Police they will be on duty to render any necessary aid or services.

From a 1942 program.

Volunteer community workers posed with Orchestra members during the coupon sales campaign of 1956. The musicians were (*left to right*) Perry Crafton, Ralph Johnson, Alfred Kovar, Philip Farkas, and Robert Alexa.

67

Luciano Berio was a visitor in 1967, and Chicago composer Ralph Shapey brought his Contemporary Chamber Players ensemble in 1968.

In 1961 Monteux, who was to die (at 89) three years later, made his final Ravinia appearances two decades after his debut. As I said farewell, I called him, as always, "Papa" Monteux. "No," he chided, "now you must call me 'Grandpapa' Monteux."

With the close of the 1963 season, unable to define his role at Ravinia to his satisfaction, Hendl resigned from his post to concentrate on conducting. Whether or not you were surprised when the job went to Seiji Ozawa depended on whether or not you were at Ravinia July 18, 1963, when the twenty-seven-year-old Japanese conductor made his Chicago Symphony debut, replacing the ailing Georges Prêtre. His training, under Bernstein at Tanglewood and Herbert von Karajan in Berlin, was demonstrated in secure orchestral control, and his energy, his ear for tonal color, and his power to persuade were undeniable. In the final days of August he was named music director and conductor for three summers beginning in 1964.

Helen Tieken Geraghty was hired as the Festival's first general manager in 1964 and served through 1965, but her experience was producing pageants, not concerts. She will be best remembered for her role in presenting the Shakespeare festival, which Chairman Earle Ludgin organized in 1964 around a group of imported British actors directed by Peter Dews.

An experienced music manager, Marshall Turkin, was engaged as general manager in 1966. A Chicagoan, he came to Ravinia after managing the symphony orchestras of Fort Wayne and Honolulu. An advisory Music Committee, headed by George Howerton, dean of the School of Music at Northwestern University, was created to "submit suitable soloists, conductors, and programs."

In two years with Turkin the Ravinia schedule departed from its traditional pattern. The "Mondays at the Murray" became a showcase for recitals; jazz and folk music were shifted to the Wednesday and Friday slots. Tuesdays became nights for special events, light or serious, and the symphony concerts dominated the weekend when the largest audiences were generally available. Working from this new format, Edward Gordon, and later Gordon and James Levine, moved into the fluid program planning that marks Ravinia today, in which diversification and integration are central themes.

Ozawa quickly emerged as a leader. From his first program, he showed a deep commitment to 20th-century music, including the composers of his native Japan. Sunday afternoon concerts, which had been abandoned in 1959 because of weak attendance, were restored and by 1967 Ozawa made them the most exciting, if not the best attended, events on the summer schedule. In this setting he presented the music he personally most wanted to play, concentrating on the present century, but he insisted that his long-term goal was what he called "mixed" programming, in which Berg and Beethoven might stand together, an objective that has been achieved in the Levine years.

Among the works Gunther Schuller conducted at Ravinia were two world premieres in 1970: his own Suite from *The Visitation* and Easley Blackwood's Piano Concerto, with the composer as soloist.

The popular Spanish pianist and conductor José Iturbi made several visits to the Festival. He is shown here trying out a piano for performances of works by George Gershwin and Manuel de Falla in 1962.

Seiji Ozawa, music director of the Ravinia Festival from 1964 to 1968, and principal conductor in 1969.

While his colleague Robert Craft rehearses the CSO onstage, Igor Stravinsky follows the score from his seat in the Pavilion, flanked by Seiji Ozawa and a friend.

Shown here during a 1966 Ravinia engagement under Seiji Ozawa's direction, Van Cliburn performed the Tchaikovsky Piano Concerto No. 1 and the Beethoven *Emperor* Concerto.

French conductor and composer Jean Martinon led the Orchestra at Ravinia in 1960 and 1962, prior to his appointment as the seventh music director of the Chicago Symphony (1963–1967). His Cello Concerto, Op. 52 was given its United States premiere at Ravinia in 1965, with soloist Janos Starker.

No visitor was received with greater enthusiasm during the Ozawa summers than Igor Stravinsky, who was present in four years, 1962 to 1965, with his associate Robert Craft. His first concert drew an audience of 10,241, a new record for a Chicago Symphony program. Although musically memorable, these events generated a certain amount of friction offstage over recording sessions. Stravinsky had fights with the Orchestra and the critics, and his final appearances downtown in the holiday weeks of 1966–67 were not a happy farewell for someone who had done so much for music.

The unique charm of the Ozawa summers was, in the largest sense, the warm personal appeal of "Seiji san," young, talented, relaxed, dedicated to music, and, obviously, on the brink of a great career that has reached its fulfillment since his Ravinia years. He worked hard, and he played hard. A Saturday night that began with a concert at Ravinia might end with his white Mustang convertible heading south to Chicago where he would relax and listen to jazz until the early hours. The Orchestra respected him, and he was never slow to express his admiration for the musicians he led. It was a love match that went on for five years. But he was anxious to avail himself of every opportunity to grow professionally, and in 1969 when offered a chance to expand his experience by directing a fully staged opera at the Salzburg Festival, Ozawa asked to be released from the final year of his second Ravinia contract. The 1969 season found him briefly in residence as a principal guest conductor, but the future belonged to others.

Important as he was, Ozawa was not the only significant figure in the Ravinia of the 1960s. Jean Martinon, who was to succeed Reiner downtown, was a guest in 1960, 1962, and 1967. Martinon's teacher Charles Munch, the finest French conductor of the generation following Monteux, was on hand for 1966 and 1967. André Previn first came in 1964, and the following summer introduced Georges Prêtre. Unforgettable too were the programs in 1967, when Sir Malcolm Sargent, tall, tanned, and elegant in a tailcoat, led the Orchestra in some of his long-established specialties. Few suspected that he was gravely ill and would die in the early autumn.

Ravinia has, over the years, had many Viennese nights, but none to surpass those of 1963, 1965, and 1968, when the soloist was Elisabeth Schwarzkopf and the conductor Willi Boskovsky, concertmaster of the Vienna Philharmonic, who led the Orchestra Johann Strauss-style, violin in hand, using his bow as the baton. In 1966 Henry Lewis, a pioneer black conductor, made his debut. He was to return in 1968 and 1975.

The far-reaching change that was to shape the future came in March 1968, when Turkin departed to take over the Blossom Music Center of the Cleveland Orchestra and Edward Gordon, a respected pianist who had turned to management in 1958 and headed the free Chicago concerts of the Grant Park Symphony since 1962, came to Ravinia. The front office was now occupied by a musician who was also a good businessman. Gordon had a fresh point of view. He also had a mandate from the Ravinia board, and particularly its chairman Stanley M. Freehling, to "turn things around," a phrase that, in practical terms, meant bringing the highest level of professionalism to the operations of the Festival. The enlarged scope of Gordon's responsibilities made the continuation of the Music Committee unnecessary.

Gordon's first season had been planned largely by his predecessor, which gave him an opportunity to observe how things went. A number of established practices, he decided, had nothing to recommend them except tradition, and they were quickly modernized. Gordon looked for a public more representative of the community as a whole, most significantly a public in which a great many persons would without strain cross over from popular music to the classics and vice versa. If you offered programs that appealed to a variety of tastes, a person who first came to Ravinia for one sort of attraction might return for other types of music.

Ravinia was already committed to diversified programming. Moderate rock, as represented by such groups as The Association, The Mob, and Harper's Bizarre, had been offered in 1967 and 1968. In 1969 Ravinia added hard rock music to its offerings with a committee of young people assisting in the selection of the most popular groups, opening with Iron Butterfly and the Mothers of Invention. A delayed arrival in 1970 by Motown star Dionne Warwick precipitated what was called a "mini-riot" and produced strained relations with those who lived on the streets surrounding the park. In consequence, there was concern among the members of the Executive Committee about the scheduled appearance of Janis Joplin, one of the chief exponents of the rebellious spirit of the times. But when she came to Ravinia that summer (drawing a huge crowd that required extra police to keep things in hand) there were no incidents.

Jesus Christ Superstar attracted a vast audience in 1971, spreading the smell of pot over the park like incense in a church. But that was the end. Ravinia was not prepared to deal with audiences of the size and temperament that the rock concert phenomenon produced, and the experiment was brought to a close, although some carefully selected attractions (such as Jackson Browne in 1978) have continued to draw huge audiences. Innovative popular music, especially that of jazz and folk artists, remains a basic part of the Festival. Indeed, Ravinia, in some ways, is several festivals all going on at the same time and attracting multiple audiences, some participating in a variety of events, others staying with their particular interests. The remarkable thing is that there appears to be plenty going on to keep them all happy.

From the outset, Gordon concerned himself with long-term planning. Although the new seats installed in 1949 were of high quality, conditions backstage were poor and the stage itself remained the temporary structure hastily built after the fire. Working with a Forward Planning Committee, Gordon devised a model plan for development of buildings and artistic programs and raising the required funds. The dramatic outcome of this, in the summer of 1970, was a modern stage with a dance

A well-known leader of the American folksong revival, Pete Seeger is a laureate of six Ravinia summers since the nation's Bicentennial year. His sentiments: "Keep Ravinia reaching out to all kinds of people. Our greatest songs are yet unsung."

In 1970, in one of her last performances, Janis Joplin belted the blues in her signature style at Ravinia.

Dave Brubeck offered the following anecdote: "My debut at Ravinia was in 1953. The Festival had had great artistic and public success, but financially needed a fund-raiser to insure the following season. I agreed to play two concerts for a very small fee. When I arrived in Chicago, I was summoned to a meeting of the Board of Directors, held in a large downtown bank. I was sternly warned that if there were any 'jitterbugging' in the aisles (as had evidently happened years before when they had 'taken a chance' on Benny Goodman) my concert would be immediately canceled. Fortunately there was no jitterbugging, but the audience was so large that a traffic cop described it as 'the biggest crowd to leave Chicago since the Fire'. I have since returned many times."

Openness to innovation has resulted in unusual concert settings as well as new programming concepts. A Mozart Marathon made use of the Gazebo (ordinarily a food facility) for a program by some of the Chicago Symphony wind players.

The first "concert previews," an innovation of the Gordon/Levine team, took place in the Pavilion. Here James Levine and John Browning perform Brahms's Variations on a Theme by Haydn.

Mutual admiration sparks the relationship between Ravinia and twelve-season laureate André Watts, who first appeared at the Festival in 1965, two years after his New York debut at age sixteen with Leonard Bernstein. Watts recalls: "I have had so many delightful experiences at Ravinia that whenever I return for a concert I feel as if I'm going to my own musical summer-cottage for a vacation. The combination of informality at rehearsal and serious musical intent is something that makes performances with Levine and the Chicagoans a special joy."

"I don't want to celebrate the Rachmaninoff piano concerti every year," Levine announced. Gordon had, from the start, searched for a mixture of established artists and noteworthy young musicians. One goes to Ravinia to hear both the stars of today and the probable stars of tomorrow. The repertory has been founded on a desire to reach and please a variety of tastes. Ideally it was to be a finely balanced mixture of summer staples plus a number of works that would be unusual under any circumstances.

In looking at Levine's programs for a dozen summers, one notes that they range from Bach to Xenakis and that he has offered a fairly comprehensive survey of the important orchestral literature from 1775 to 1925. Instead of merely repeating scores, he has regularly offered music that he has not conducted at Ravinia before. But Levine's work at Ravinia has not been limited to conducting. As he saw it, the chamber music programs at the Murray provided an essential artistic contrast to the orchestral concerts, and Levine has been active in both series. His contributions and repertory as a pianist are as impressive as his work with the Orchestra.

A third important aspect of the Ravinia schedule, as Levine and Gordon saw it, was an educational program involving artists who could stay in residence a few days and offer master classes as well as appear before the public. Committees responsible for forward planning had made such a recommendation as early as 1961 and again in 1968, but it had been impossible to implement it then. Master classes began in cooperation with the summer program of the Northwestern University School of Music in 1972. This was a foundation on which to build.

It would be reasonable to assume that a festival that has as its music director the artistic head of the Metropolitan Opera would consider becoming an opera producer again. On the other hand, for both aesthetic and economic reasons, the Ravinia Opera of the early years of the century could not be revived in the 1970s. Fully staged works were, for the immediate future, out of the question. Ravinia had attempted opera in concert as early as 1954, when Monteux directed Gounod's *Faust*. Opera flourished again in the summer of 1969 with presentations of Puccini's *Madama Butterfly* under the direction of Alain Lombard and Verdi's *Aida*, directed by Giuseppe Patanè. Kertész did two more Verdi scores, *Rigoletto* and *Otello*, in concert form, as well as Béla Bartók's *Duke Bluebeard's Castle*. Levine and Gordon searched for operas that made effective use of the potential of the Chicago Symphony and could be projected effectively in purely musical terms. Berlioz's *Les Troyens* was such a work. Levine offered it in concert form in 1978, anticipating his revival of the opera for the centennial season of the Metropolitan in 1983. Three Verdi scores, *La Traviata* in 1974, *La Forza del Destino* in 1979, and *Macbeth* in 1981, proved unusually successful in a concert setting.

If Ravinia remains primarily the summer residence of the Chicago Symphony, it has also, since the mid-1960s, been host to other orchestras. In

Soloists Shirley Verrett, Guy Chauvet, Claudine Carlson, David Kuebler, Ara Berberian, and John Cheek in a 1978 performance of *Les Troyens*. The monumental five-act Berlioz opera, based on Virgil's *Aeneid*, was finally published in its entirety during the composer's centenary in 1969. Ravinia presented the historic Chicago premiere in two parts on successive evenings.

Cellist Janos Starker (*left*) and violinist Itzhak Perlman (*below, at right*) were among the first artist-teachers to offer master classes at Ravinia under the auspices of the Festival and the Northwestern University School of Music. The program was begun in 1972.

A 1976 piano master class with Rudolf Firkušný shows the participants in the intimate setting of the old Casino building, which also housed art exhibits.

1967 Yehudi Menuhin brought the Bath Festival Orchestra to Ravinia, followed the next summer by the English Chamber Orchestra conducted by Daniel Barenboim. The London Symphony has played Ravinia twice, led by André Previn in 1969 and by Neville Marriner in 1982; Zubin Mehta brought the New York Philharmonic in 1981; and the Cleveland Orchestra had a weekend at Ravinia, Eduardo Mata conducting, in 1983. Since 1982 The Saint Paul Chamber Orchestra led by Pinchas Zukerman, its music director, has had the final spot in the summer calendar.

The paradox of the Levine seasons is that not infrequently he has prepared as many different programs with the Chicago Symphony during the course of three or four weeks of summer residence as Sir Georg Solti, its music director since 1969, prepares in an entire Orchestra Hall season. Solti, of course, has the advantage of more extensive rehearsal time, and he must play each program in two or three subscription series—and possibly on tour. His total number of performances, and his total number of hours with the Orchestra each year, exceed those of his Ravinia colleague. But from the point of view of developing a bond of understanding between a conductor and a group of musicians, the two situations have much in common. It is precisely by working through a large body of music literature, scores in different styles from different periods, that musicians and conductors get to know one another with the fullness of understanding that leads to distinguished performances. Once Levine had this exposure, its cumulative effect quickly be-

The New York Philharmonic, with Zubin Mehta, performed Stravinsky's *The Rite of Spring,* Brahms's Third Symphony, and works by Beethoven, Vieuxtemps, and Mussorgsky during the Festival's 1981 season.

André Previn during rehearsal for his Ravinia appearances with the Chicago Symphony in 1976.

Isaac Stern and Pinchas Zukerman performing Mozart's Sinfonia Concertante, K. 364, with The Saint Paul Chamber Orchestra in 1983.

lon have both figured in the roster for a number of years. Michael Tilson Thomas, who made his Ravinia debut in 1970, returned in 1982, 1983, and 1984. A major young British talent, Simon Rattle, was a visitor in 1979. David Zinman, heard at Ravinia in 1974, went on to become a major force in the free concerts of Chicago's Grant Park Symphony. Riccardo Muti, who was to succeed Ormandy with the Philadelphia Orchestra, was at Ravinia in 1973.

Leinsdorf, one of the few links to the first years of the Festival, was back in 1976 and 1980. Kurt Masur, representing the older European generation, appeared in 1981, 1982, and 1984, and Edo de Waart, one of Europe's most important conductors of Levine's age group, came to Ravinia in 1971 and marked his fifth summer in 1983. Neville Marriner was a visitor in 1980, 1981, and 1982. Maxim Shostakovich established himself on the Ravinia calendar with three appearances from 1982 to 1984. And even those who were present for a single summer left some strong impressions, particularly Mstislav Rostropovich in 1975 and Marek Janowski in 1982. Illustrious conductors were matched with equally illustrious soloists, many of whom are pictured in these pages.

"Pops" concerts are nothing new for Ravinia. Arthur Fiedler, who made the Boston Pops a national institution, first appeared at the Festival in 1954 and returned as his schedule and health permitted. In the Levine seasons he was on hand in 1973, 1974, and 1976. His death in 1979 left a gap that no one was quite prepared to fill. Both John

Edo de Waart, who made his CSO debut at Ravinia in 1971, is shown at rehearsal during the 1983 season. The Dutch-born conductor will become music director of the Netherlands Opera in 1985, following an eight-year tenure as music director of the San Francisco Symphony.

Edward Gordon and Michael Tilson Thomas in conversation backstage. Mr. Thomas first conducted the Chicago Symphony during Ravinia's 1970 season with repertoire that included Varèse's *Intégrales*.

James Conlon, music director of the Rotterdam Philharmonic and regular Festival guest since 1977, recalls: "The summer of Ravinia's Mahler cycle in which I conducted the CSO in the Fifth Symphony stands out in my memory. When I first heard the CSO live at Carnegie Hall in the late 1960s they gave that work an unforgettable performance. I could scarcely imagine that eight years later Ravinia would offer me the privilege of conducting that Orchestra, or that in just two years more I would conduct the very work that had left such an indelible impression. At Ravinia the combined talents of Gordon, Levine, and the CSO make possible the highest level of artistic pursuit."

Neville Marriner, music director of the Minnesota Orchestra and widely known for his many recordings with the Academy of St. Martin-in-the-Fields, has conducted the Chicago Symphony and the London Symphony at Ravinia.

Erich Leinsdorf at Ravinia in 1976. He returned in 1980, and that year he shared some of his views on music with the audience in a pre-concert talk in the Murray Theatre.

The pioneer of symphonic "pops" concerts in America, Arthur Fiedler made his first Ravinia appearance in 1954 and returned for eight more seasons. His last Ravinia concert was given in 1976, three years before his death at the age of eighty-three.

Franz Allers has brought his noted interpretations of Viennese light opera and American musical theater to Ravinia a dozen times since 1969. He gained renown, and two "Tony" awards, for his conducting of the original productions of *My Fair Lady* and *Camelot*.

89

Above: Conductor Erich Kunzel, who sent these anniversary greetings: "To every Ravinia concert-goer, my hat is off to you — often one sees the champagne flowing, the candelabra lit, the gourmet food baskets, and the good cheer and happiness of all attending this great festival. But the prize for all is the music. From Bach to Bartók, from symphony to jazz, from recitalists to folk, from ballet to blues, it is all there—it is Ravinia!" *Right*: A popular moment that has become the traditional close of the Chicago Symphony's annual Festival residency: a battery of cannons augments the Orchestra in Tchaikovsky's *1812* Overture.

Symphonic "pops" concerts at Ravinia often bring unusual moments in a traditional concert setting—Sarah Vaughan's artistry takes a solo flight while conductor Erich Kunzel joins the audience in admiration.

Green and Franz Allers have made noteworthy contributions to establishing a lighter classical series at Ravinia, but Erich Kunzel has been the chief exponent of popular symphonic music at the Festival. In 1984 he marked his seventh consecutive summer as a dominant figure in the lighter repertory, and he has made the final symphony program of the summer, a Tchaikovsky spectacular with the *1812* Overture, cannons and all, a tradition of sorts.

In a recent conversation, Levine was at once practical and philosophical:

At Ravinia we have one of the world's greatest orchestras playing in an outdoor pavilion which has very good acoustics and a wonderful stage but is nonetheless subject to the weather. The Orchestra and I are playing three concerts a week on between four and five rehearsals—the same amount of rehearsal time given to a single program downtown. For this reason I think it would be completely wrong for Ravinia to gamble on things which are really the province of the winter season concerts.

I was in my twenties when I first came to Ravinia, and the opportunity to work with an orchestra of the stature of the Chicago Symphony was exhilarating. Now I am past forty, and I want the opportunity to work with some kind of depth, which you can't do without repetition, a chance to go at a thing again. So there may be fewer examples of reckless abandon, but the music is better. I think this is truly the time we look at things in terms of longer perspectives and goals. I think the more we integrate what goes on in the Murray Theatre with what goes on in the Pavilion, the more we get an educational structure together, the more we can build a foundation for the present Ravinia that is as strong as the opera in the old Pavilion was for the old Ravinia.

Ravinia has an enormous potential. By continuing to take risks with innovative programming and making the best use of the talent available to us each summer—seasoned performers as well as young artists in the early stages of their careers—we can develop new levels of performance.

Under Levine and Gordon, both of whom speak for themselves elsewhere in this volume, Ravinia has become one of the most successful and significant summer music series in the world. But both men see the development of the Festival as a continuing process. Each summer's successes point the way to new lines of exploration and fresh possibilities. The most exciting thing about Ravinia is that its potential is still being developed and every year is an invitation to discovery and new victories.

91

AN ILLUSTRATED INTERLUDE

Standing ovations greeted Aaron Copland, the "dean of American composers," during his 1982 return to Ravinia as narrator for his *Lincoln Portrait*, with Erich Kunzel conducting. (At Copland's 1956 Festival debut, when he conducted his own works, the *Portrait* had been narrated by actor Claude Rains.) Said Copland during his recent visit: "I retain many happy memories of my several past visits as conductor at the annual Ravinia Festival. The Orchestra has always been warmly responsive to the works we have performed together. The outdoor setting of the Festival is in itself a stimulus to doing one's best for a very receptive audience."

The following pages offer glimpses of the great variety of activities in music, dance, theater, and the visual arts that have distinguished the Festival in recent years. If the Ravinia of the 1920s was known for the splendor of its opera, the Festival has come to be known for a whole range of programming in addition to its presentation of classical music as performed by the Chicago Symphony Orchestra and Chorus, occasional visiting orchestras, and a great many visiting artists. Performed in the Pavilion or the more intimate Murray Theatre, this remains Ravinia's glory, but as this pictorial interlude shows, Ravinia has also offered its audiences some of the finest dance companies of our time; some of our greatest jazz, folk, and popular music performers; and plays ancient and modern, from Shakespeare to Tennessee Williams. And all of this has taken place in a setting that elicited from the wife of composer-conductor Paul Hindemith the joyous exclamation: "Everywhere I look I see Renoirs!"

Peter Serkin at Ravinia in 1978. He first appeared at the Festival as a young artist of nineteen in 1965, returning for six more seasons, most recently in 1984.

Father and son, Robert and Nicholas Mann, presented a program of Bartók duos in 1977.

In a 1974 Preview recital James Levine and the Chicago Symphony String Quartet performed Dvořák's Piano Quintet, Opus 81 before an orchestral concert that included the composer's Seventh Symphony.

Works of Grieg, Rachmaninoff, and Dvořák were offered by violinist Cho-Liang Lin, pianist Misha Dichter, and cellist Frederick Zlotkin in 1984.

Orchestral soloist, recitalist, chamber musician, artist-teacher, there is almost no role Misha Dichter has not filled in his seventeen-year association with Ravinia. "My first appearance at the Ravinia Festival with the Chicago Symphony took place in the summer of '68 in a performance of the Tchaikovsky Concerto No. 1 with Josef Krips. I remember the impressions of that first meeting with the Orchestra most vividly, as it was an almost story-book realization of a childhood dream: to make music with the Chicago Symphony!"

James Galway rehearses for his 1981 performance with the Chicago Symphony at Ravinia.

Thomas Riebl, Viennese-born winner of the 1982 Naumburg Viola Competition, rehearses with Edo de Waart and the CSO for his 1983 performance of the Bartók Viola Concerto.

95

Nadja Salerno-Sonnenberg, winner of the 1981 Naumburg Award for violin, receives a helping hand from the concertmaster's desk during a hot-weather rehearsal.

Martina Arroyo, who portrayed title roles in *Madama Butterfly* and *Aida* at Ravinia in 1969, returned in 1974 to share an evening of arias and duets with Richard Tucker and the CSO.

Cellist Yo-Yo Ma during a performance of Haydn's Cello Concerto in D Major in 1982.

Robert Mann, James Levine, Lynn Harrell, and Michael Ouzounian in a 1977 performance of Mozart's Piano Quartet in G Minor, which they later recorded for RCA's *Music from Ravinia* series.

In 1945 the seventeen-year-old Leon Fleisher performed Brahms's Piano Concerto No. 1 and Liszt's Piano Concerto No. 2 under the direction of twenty-six-year-old Leonard Bernstein. Pictured here in 1984, Mr. Fleisher had returned as an artist-in-residence, performing Ravel's Concerto for the Left Hand, and teaching a series of master classes in the Murray Theatre.

In 1979 Soviet violinist Vladimir Spivakov led a chamber orchestra of Chicago Symphony musicians in a concert of Mozart works.

Among the Beaux Arts Trio's mementos is a mid-1950s brochure quoting such Chicago headlines as "New Trio Makes Big Ravinia Cozy," that recalled the Festival's role in launching their career. Pianist Menahem Pressler and cellist Bernard Greenhouse are original ensemble members; violinist Isidore Cohen, shown here, succeeded Daniel Guilet in 1968.

During several visits to Ravinia, French flutist Jean-Pierre Rampal has performed as soloist with the Chicago Symphony, appeared in recital, and conducted master classes.

Violinist Shlomo Mintz in rehearsal at the 1982 Festival. He has been a regular guest since his impressive 1980 Ravinia debut.

The young British-born artist Stephen Hough came to Ravinia for his CSO debut after winning the 1983 Naumburg Piano Competition.

Itzhak Perlman in 1977. Recalling a much earlier performance, Perlman wrote: "I remember one of the first times I played at Ravinia. It was before the place was renovated. It was very humid and muggy. At one point I was playing the Wienawski Concerto with Sir Malcolm Sargent and I was dressed in as thin a white jacket as I could find. Sir Malcolm, however, was spiffily attired in tails that were made of a very thick material and yet there was not a drop of sweat on his brow. I always marvelled at that experience. Today, of course, the Ravinia Festival is one of the great festivals in America and the facilities (including the backstage) are great."

The LaSalle Quartet in the early 1970s: violist Peter Kamnitzer, violinists Henry Meyer and Walter Levin, and cellist Jack Kirstein. This group, especially renowned for its Grand Prix du Disque award-winning recordings of the works of Schoenberg, Berg, and Webern, presented this difficult cycle of quartets at Ravinia in 1972, in conjunction with an informative series of lecture-demonstrations on the music of these remarkable 20th-century composers.

Twenty-year-old Cecile Licad performed Chopin's Piano Concerto No. 2 at her Ravinia debut in 1982, shortly after she was awarded the prestigious Leventritt Prize.

Commenting on his appearances at Ravinia, Lorin Hollander recalled: "What stays most vividly in my memory is an evening in 1976 when I played with Jim Levine on an all-Gershwin night. There were nearly 18,000 people present, and it was a joyful and spontaneous concert experience. After the Concerto in F and the *Rhapsody in Blue* Jim invited me to play ten minutes of Gershwin piano solos as an encore, while he sat with me on the darkened stage. It was a magical moment."

Swedish baritone Håkan Hagegård was heard in three settings during his Ravinia debut season: in a lieder recital with piano, in recital with the CSO, and, with Kathleen Battle, in Brahms's *Ein Deutsches Requiem,* later a 1984 Grammy award-winning performance recorded by RCA.

Shostakovich Times Three—the composer's music conducted by his son Maxim, and with his namesake grandson Dimitri as piano soloist—was a highlight of the 1982 season. The performers are shown here rehearsing the Piano Concerto No. 1.

Pianist Alexis Weissenberg at Ravinia in 1982. During his Festival residence that season he offered a solo recital, an orchestral appearance, and master classes.

While staff and parent chaperones look on, members of the Glen Ellyn Children's Chorus sing James Levine an original song, presented "with love and admiration" in celebration of several seasons of working together. The chorus is directed by Doreen Rao.

103

Below: The cast for Mozart's *Così fan Tutte* in 1975 included Richard Stilwell, John Alexander, Roberta Peters, Patricia Wells, and Maria Ewing. The occasion is warmly remembered by Miss Peters: "It was hard to stand still with the bubbly music and Jim asked if we would like to use some props. One thing led to another and during the performance we really acted up a storm. I was disguised as 'the Doctor,' 'the Lawyer,' etc. It was great fun." *Right:* With Miss Peters (in costume) is Andrew Foldi.

Donald Gramm, Benita Valente, and Seth McCoy in rehearsal with James Levine for Haydn's *The Creation* in 1977. Mr. Gramm, who made his Ravinia debut in 1955, offered this fond reminiscence shortly before his untimely death in 1983: "What fun it is to remember the performance of *The Creation* with Jimmy when, as I began the recitative which ends with me singing the word 'worm' on a low D, I heard the everpresent North Western train approaching. I knew if it pulled in as I gave out my low D that the train would be the winner. Jimmy heard it too. So with the slightest eye contact we slowed down the preceding bars of music. The train must have been in Racine when my lovely, low 'worm' wiggled out."

Tatiana Troyanos relaxes on the grounds at Ravinia during her 1982 visit. Commenting on her Festival engagements, Miss Troyanos said: "My experience at Ravinia has been truly unique. Above all, I have felt at home, even back in 1973 with my debut as Adalgisa in *Norma*, which was also my first collaboration with James Levine. The relaxed atmosphere provides a wonderful environment in which to make music."

107

Leontyne Price (*left*), and in a 1975 Ravinia concert appearance (*above*). Miss Price also sang Leonora in *La Forza del Destino* on the Festival's 1979 opening night. She recalls: "The Chicago Symphony is a phenomenon the whole world recognizes, but the weather on that evening proved to be a phenomenon as well. The first part of the *Forza* was performed by all of us in a sweltering, humid, heat wave temperature of 95 degrees. By the beginning of my entrance to sing the aria "Pace, pace mio Dio" the temperature had dropped to a chilly 40 degrees—prompting strongly a personal desire on my part to change the lyrics of the aria to 'Heat, heat— my God!'"

Two artists whose friendship goes back to their days of working together with Toscanini and the NBC Symphony: CSO principal cellist Frank Miller (*left*) and tenor Richard Tucker. Mr. Tucker was a guest soloist at Ravinia in 1974.

A unique event in 1983 brought Luciano Pavarotti to the Pavilion for a concert to jointly benefit Ravinia Festival and Lyric Opera of Chicago. Lyric's music director Bruno Bartoletti conducted the Opera orchestra.

In a scene from *The Abduction from the Seraglio* in 1975, Blonda, sung by Ruth Welting, works her charm on Ara Berberian's Osmin.

The 1983 season brought the very special Ravinia debut of Marilyn Horne in a concert of Rossini arias, with James Levine conducting. Miss Horne had recently become the first recipient of the Rossini Medal. Recalling her debut, Miss Horne said: "Working with James Levine (and, of course, the Chicago Symphony) is always a special musical treat, and the beautiful Pavilion made it all the more wonderful. That extraordinary outdoor setting does so much for both the audience and the performer—the debut was really a thrilling event!"

109

Sherrill Milnes first sang at Ravinia as a member of the Chicago Symphony Chorus, years before gaining renown as a Metropolitan Opera artist. Recently he reminisced: "As a hometown boy (Downers Grove) it is always a special joy to sing at Ravinia. Among my many beautiful memories of the Festival I treasure particularly the performances of *Elijah, Aida, Macbeth,* and *Rigoletto.*"

Four members of the cast of *Macbeth* relax outside their dressing rooms before the concert begins. *Left to right:* Giuliano Ciannella (holding mug of tea), Philip Creech, Timothy Jenkins, and John Cheek. Mr. Cheek recalled: "Musically speaking, I grew up at Ravinia. I have sung everything from Schubert lieder to the grandest of opera in stifling heat, freezing cold, drenching downpours, and even perfect weather. But in the midst of all these variables there have been many constants: the Orchestra working miracles in amazingly little rehearsal time, Jimmy's seemingly boundless energy, and the friendly backstage atmosphere."

Renata Scotto remembers: "The Ravinia Festival was the first time I sang *Macbeth* in this country. It will always be a special memory for me." Here she is seen in a dramatic moment as Lady Macbeth. Appearing with her are Giuliano Ciannella, Gene Marie Callahan, and Sherrill Milnes.

San Francisco Ballet, caught by the
camera at Ravinia in a 1984
performance of Balanchine's *Concerto
Barocco*. The company, directed by
Michael Smuin and Lew Christensen,
first appeared at Ravinia in 1980.

The 40s, choreographed by Lou Conte for his Hubbard Street Dance Company, is representative of the group's lively style.

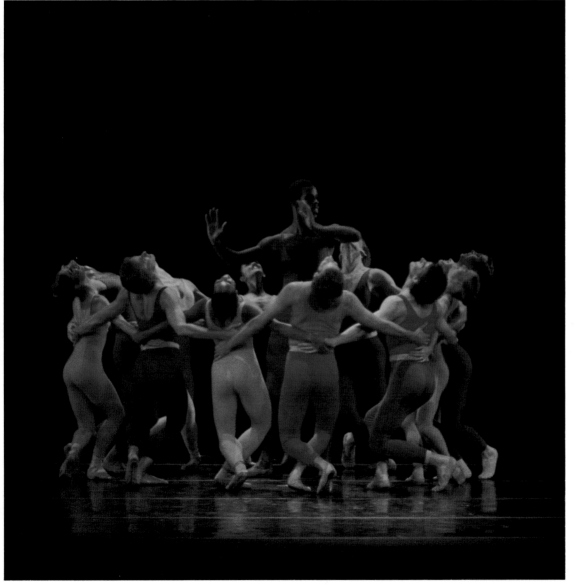

The Joffrey Ballet at Ravinia in one of the most popular rock ballets produced in America—*Trinity,* with choreography by Gerald Arpino to music by Alan Raph and Lee Holdridge.

In their 1977 appearance at Ravinia the Twyla Tharp Dance Foundation dancers performed to music that included works by Mozart, Paul Simon, Jelly Roll Morton, and Fats Waller. The 1980 program was equally varied.

Named after a "genus of phototropic fungi," the Pilobolus Dance Theatre performs works choreographed by its members, set to contemporary music.

In its Midwest debut, the Hamburg Ballet performed at Ravinia with a repertory that included Bach's *St. Matthew Passion (below)*, as well as *Mahler's Third Symphony* and a stunningly staged interpretation of *A Midsummer Night's Dream*. All three were choreographed by artistic director John Neumeier, pictured (in center) in the role of Christ. *Right:* Soloist Jeffrey Kirk.

Lively debate has surrounded the issue of integrating jazz, folk, and popular music into the Festival's regular schedule over the years. As early as 1938, when Benny Goodman was invited for a special engagement, Festival trustees correctly surmised that such revenues could help support other artistic goals, but general acceptance of popular artists on Ravinia's stage was slow in coming. During the 1950s audiences were actually polled; while many welcomed the idea, others, like the author of the following comment from a 1954 postcard, were distinctly opposed: "I hope you do not turn over this beautiful spot for Jazz Programs. There are plenty of other places for this sort of thing. Let this place alone."

By the late 1960s, however, as the Festival grew more assured about the planning of popular events, non-classical music became a frequent feature of the Ravinia season. In the last fifteen years alone, well over 100 different jazz, folk, or popular groups have appeared at Ravinia. The performers ranged from Indian sitar master Ravi Shankar to blues guitarist B. B. King, from The Limeliters to Frank Zappa and The Mothers of Invention, from Victor Borge to Ramsey Lewis. But the purpose behind the selection remains consistent—to present artists whose work is classic in its genre.

Louis "Satchmo" Armstrong was an early guest among popular artists. He first came in 1956, then returned three more times before the end of his career; he died in 1971.

Dionne Warwick in a 1980 Festival photo, ten years after her first engagement.

118

Two performances of the rock opera *Jesus Christ Superstar* were presented in semi-staged concert performance at Ravinia in 1971.

Ella Fitzgerald is the "first lady of song" at Ravinia, as she is all around the world. In 1983 Miss Fitzgerald marked the 20th anniversary of her first Ravinia appearance, and she continues to be a regular guest.

Peter, Paul and Mary, a group welcomed warmly by Ravinia audiences both in the late 1960s and in their reunion appearances in the 1980s.

119

Tales are still told of the box office lines for Barry Manilow's concerts at Ravinia in the mid-1970s. Ravinia provided a lasting memory for Manilow as well: "Not only did I enjoy the beautiful atmosphere at Ravinia but the live portions of my first TV special were taped during my appearance there in 1976. It was definitely a magical evening for myself, my crew, my band, Lady Flash, and my audience. I remember we stayed late into the evening taping the show and I don't think any members of the audience left or lost any of their enthusiasm. Thanks to Ravinia I have a big shiny Emmy on my mantel to remind me of that special evening."

Harry Chapin was due to arrive at Ravinia in July of 1981 when news of his accidental death saddened the nation. He had been a guest at Ravinia for three consecutive years beginning in 1976.

The spirit of New Orleans is transplanted to Chicago nearly every summer with the arrival of the Preservation Hall Jazz Band at Ravinia.

Tina Turner, with the Ike and Tina Turner Revue, was an electrifying performer during the 1971 and 1972 seasons.

Since 1970 Judy Collins's Festival appearances have drawn a loyal following. Long-stemmed red roses (*at right*) are Ravinia's traditional tribute before her final encore. In a return tribute to Ravinia, Miss Collins writes: "At Ravinia the nights and the music and the people have been a high point of my touring every year for more than a decade. From the first time I performed on that magnificent stage I felt that the theater in the summer air was my home."

Sounds of the Big Band era are popular among Ravinia audiences of nearly every age. Shown here are Tex Beneke (*in white coat*), Helen Forrest (*center*), Johnny Desmond (*far left*), and Paula Kelly, Jr. and the Modernaires in their "Summer of '42" evening.

Harry Belafonte made his first appearance at Ravinia in 1983.

New to the Ravinia calendar in 1984 was "classic" song stylist Tony Bennett.

122

Melissa Manchester was a guest in 1977, 1980, and 1981. She wrote: "It has always been a pleasure to work at Ravinia Festival because of the wonderful staff, beautiful surroundings, and the enthusiastic people of Chicago."

Trumpeter Wynton Marsalis, equally well known in jazz and classical music genres, made his Festival debut in 1984 with a jazz program in the Pavilion. The other band member pictured is Marsalis's brother, Branford.

Irene Dailey and Dan O'Herlihy as Eliza and W. O. Gant in Ketti Frings's adaptation of Thomas Wolfe's *Look Homeward, Angel*, performed at Ravinia in 1971.

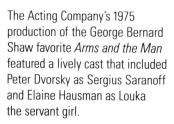

The Acting Company's 1975 production of the George Bernard Shaw favorite *Arms and the Man* featured a lively cast that included Peter Dvorsky as Sergius Saranoff and Elaine Hausman as Louka the servant girl.

The Acting Company's Kevin Kline (*left*) and Patti LuPone (*in circle*) played the lead roles in the 1975 production of *The Robber Bridegroom* by Alfred Uhry, based on a novella by Eudora Welty.

Accompanied by his brother Dakin, playwright Tennessee Williams (*below right*) attended a Ravinia performance of his *Camino Real* (a scene of which appears above right) in 1977. The cast included Mary Lou Rosato as The Gypsy and James Harper as Kilroy.

The 1975 repertory of The Acting Company included Christopher Marlowe's *Edward II*. In the foreground of this dramatic scene are Mary Joan Negro and Norman Snow.

John Houseman, a founder and
the artistic director of The Acting
Company, directed the production
of Marc Blitzstein's *The Cradle
Will Rock* at Ravinia in 1983.
Left: Houseman at work.
Below: The ensemble in action.

There was always more to a Ravinia evening than music. The progression that led, over the years, to the diversified food services that characterize the Ravinia of the 1980s began in 1943 when hot food was offered in the old carousel for the first time. A steam table was installed and roast beef, pasta (with a special sauce devised by park manager John Laurie), and staples such as beans, chili, and hot dogs were offered to hungry music lovers. During the same summer picnic tables fabricated from the doors of old costume lockers from the opera years were installed.

In observing the people who come to Ravinia, I have found that the basic difference between those who sit on the lawn and those who sit in the Pavilion is in their point of view of what constitutes the Festival experience. Those sitting in the Pavilion listen to live music from the stage; those on the lawn listen to a mixture of live and amplified sounds, the exact ratio depending on where they are sitting. People who sit in the Pavilion can always be identified on their arrival at the park by the fact that their hands are empty. Those who sit on the lawn, by contrast, may be nearly buried under deck chairs, picnic baskets, wine coolers, and similar gear. People heading for the Pavilion are going to a concert. If the concert is to be prefaced by a meal, it will be in a restaurant. People seeking out their space on the lawn have a much wider range of anticipation. They are going to regale themselves in the pleasures of a summer night, eat, drink, converse with family and friends, and, finally, have their spirits lifted by sweet harmonies.—R.C.M.

Amid the white oak, maple, ash, and linden trees stands the Pavilion, with a fan-shaped roof that rests on a peristyle of twenty columns and "floats" forty-odd feet above the audience. The audience space is defined by a canopy of lights and clusters of lights on the surrounding pillars, with illuminated trees at the perimeter.

When Ravinia opened it was a handsome green park in a rural setting. Today it is a Festival within the urban area in which the Orchestra plays its subscription concerts downtown from September to June, but at Ravinia there are more young people both for the symphony concerts and the lighter music programs that round out the schedule, and it appeals to any who prefer to listen to music in a more casual setting than the concert hall provides. Ravinia is at least thirty percent a state of mind, best regarded as a civilized place in which to enjoy the unique pleasures of a glorious summer night, to hear Mozart from the lawn with a glass of wine, or to sit inside the spacious and comfortable Pavilion in a more formal manner.

It is the nature of Ravinia that those on the lawn are the majority. The Pavilion can't possibly bring in enough income to sustain the Festival, and it is the dominant role of the lawn audience that largely defines the informal atmosphere of the concerts.—R.C.M.

When the day's rehearsals end the gates open to Ravinia-goers who arrive early with picnic baskets, blankets, and chairs to seek a favorite place on the lawn for dining and listening to the evening's program. Begonias, petunias, cleome, lilies, and hydrangea planted against the backdrop of trees complement the colors of their summer apparel.

133

On the west side of the meadow is a modern restaurant facility, offering buffets, take-out fare, and full-service dining.

Margaret McClure (*left*), now a life trustee, has been an active volunteer throughout the Festival's history. She presides over the park's landscaping—care of the planted gardens, walkways, and meadows—assisted in recent years by fellow gardener and current Ravinia president Ilo Harris.

A view of one of the park's picnic areas through the surrounding trees.

Just inside the original Ravinia gate stands the 923-seat Murray Theatre, with its twin towers, gable roof, and lanterns gracing the entryway. Inside, art nouveau chandeliers illuminate the Tiffany windows as well as the intricately stenciled ceiling.

The Gazebo, located close to the Pavilion, offers elegant boxed suppers for impromptu picnics.

135

Reflections on Making Music at Ravinia

BY JAMES LEVINE

A festival has always meant something very significant to me—an atmosphere of excitement, a special working relationship among the artists, a sense of community between artist and audience so that the interchange between the creative effort and the audience is very strong—a listening, learning, working, rejuvenating experience!

One doesn't encounter this special atmosphere often, but it *is* something I grew up with at the Aspen Festival in the late '50s and early '60s. The whole town seemed given over to the music festival; students, teachers, performers practicing and rehearsing all over town. Shopkeepers knew all the students, many by name. Everybody lived, worked, and relaxed together in this most unusual environment. A lot of unfamiliar music by familiar composers, familiar music by unfamiliar composers, and music for every conceivable combination of instruments and voices was performed. This kind of summer—studying, hearing, and performing a highly concentrated and closely related program of great music in a uniquely beautiful natural setting—was an indescribable pleasure.

The Aspen Festival has changed very much in twenty-five years, but its original premise is still valid today. At Ravinia, we have the beautiful setting of Ravinia Park and we have the Chicago Symphony Orchestra—one of the world's greatest, with outstanding individual solo players—as the splendid artistic nucleus of the Festival. The Chicago Symphony Chorus is in residence for large and small choral works; the artists-in-residence, many of whom return year after year, add cohesion and unity. This gives us a great opportunity to broaden the repertoire in a stimulating way by relating performances of orchestral music to performances of chamber music and lieder, and by using the talents of the soloists together with my own and those of the members of the Orchestra in various combinations. In effect then, we have a "faculty" which offers a kind of performing and educational continuum, both for the artists and for the audience.

The surprisingly large and consistently faithful audience at Ravinia seems to appreciate this new dimension, and gets very involved personally and musically as they understand more intimately each individual performer's musical personality.

Two of the Festival's regularly
returning artists-in-residence, violinist
Christian Altenburger and violist
Michael Ouzounian, rehearse for a
performance of Mozart's *Sinfonia
Concertante*, K. 364.

Schubert's *Trout* Quintet, as performed by Christian Altenburger, James Levine, James Kreger, Michael Ouzounian, and Joseph Guastafeste in 1984.

Edward Gordon practices for a 1978 performance of Mozart's "Ch'io mi scordi di te" with soprano Jessye Norman and the CSO.

The wonderful facilities of the park itself—the Pavilion for orchestral and choral/orchestral music and dance; the Murray Theatre for recitals, chamber music, plays and master classes; the pleasant dining facilities used by performers and audience, and, of course, the ambience of the beautiful trees, open space, and fresh air—all add to the infinite possibilities for a festival, despite the theoretical drawback of its location in a working, year-round community instead of the usual resort or vacation environment.

Ravinia is also a place where I find in the executive director, Edward Gordon, someone who understands my point of view, who understands what kind of a festival idea I am trying to achieve, and who helps me every step of the way and stimulates me in directions which I don't generate on my own. For one thing, he is himself such a fabulous and experienced pianist (he has been a soloist with the Chicago Symphony both downtown and at Ravinia) that he has gained respect from his colleagues as a first-class performer. This makes an enormous difference. The Orchestra members and soloists feel he can understand the problems and appreciate the difficulties. He can smell potential crises before they happen, and improve the conditions and eliminate the distractions as cleverly as has ever been done. Ours is a wonderful relationship and, as I've said before, the chance to work on this kind of level in a summer festival is extraordinary.

Actually, I'm astonished when I see what a short number of weeks in just a handful of summers can add up to in performance quality and program diversity. What's different about Ravinia is the marked change of pace, both for the artists and for the audience. It has something to do with having this very great orchestra play so much music close together, interacting with small music, chamber music, all close together. It is the proximity of the music to itself which is so fascinating to me. When you buy a subscription to a winter series of symphony concerts, even if you go every week, you hear one program each week. This means that from the performance of one Mozart work, let us say, to another, may be a matter of weeks or months. Now, only an avid music lover who also goes to the string quartet series, or the piano recital series, or the series of this or that at the university gets the kind

The night before her 1976
performance with the Orchestra in
Berlioz's *The Damnation of Faust*
(with Kenneth Riegel, below), Régine
Crespin appeared with James Levine
in a Preview recital of songs by
Debussy, Duparc, Poulenc, and
Brahms (*right*).

of involvement he would get if he were an avid theater-goer, reader, or museum-goer.

At Ravinia, with three different orchestral programs and often two chamber or recital evenings and/or previews each week, we try to program around a unifying idea. For instance, we've had seasons based on the work of two or three "featured composers" or a "featured style." With this format an audience can hear in a single week everything from large choral-orchestral pieces to symphonies, to concerti, to sonatas, quartets, and songs by a specific composer. Over the whole length of the Festival, it is possible to hear a substantial number of that composer's works in all forms, both familiar and unfamiliar. The very popular "marathons" condense this format even more. Previews have been added in order to include pieces which either supplement the composer's and/or the soloist's versatility, or enhance the context of a specific piece on a given program, such as the performance of the original Brahms G Minor Quartet followed later that evening by Schoenberg's orchestral transcription of the same quartet.

Of course, all this music has to be rehearsed in the amount of time that a single winter season program would normally receive. This requires careful planning and a rethinking of the usual rehearsal techniques. Over the years of doing different styles in different ways—a new work in a lot of rehearsal time, a familiar work in a short time, a work prepared several times over several seasons, a work rehearsed for the most subtle nuances—one eventually arrives at a relationship to an orchestra as a

James Levine and Lynn Harrell rehearse Beethoven sonatas in the Murray Theatre. Harrell's earliest Ravinia performance dates back to 1966, and he has been an integral part of the Festival community since then. In his words: "Ravinia memories? Jimmy's red towel, the sense of coming home to a family, picnics, ice-cream, smiles on the lawn—and, always, the satisfaction of making marvelous music with friends and a great orchestra."

group that has its own vitality, its own mutual respect, its own affections, its own warmth. Over the years I've seen it happen. I've now passed my fiftieth performance with the Chicago Symphony Chorus. With all the enthusiasm and discipline, with all the knowledge of language its members have, with all the responsiveness Margaret Hillis's training has produced, those qualities keep getting better year after year after year—vocally better, interpretively better, more responsive.

I can see an interesting thing happening. It used to be that the Chorus' overriding strength was in the whole range of their classical repertoire. If you wanted to do an opera chorus from *Macbeth*, or a French symphony-oratorio like Berlioz's *Romeo*, or a coloristic, dramatic cantata like *Carmina Burana*, it would not have been, perhaps, quite so exciting as their Bach, Haydn, Beethoven, or Brahms. But that has gradually changed. They've gotten used to what I'm going to ask of them, and have been able to absorb some of the freedom and expression of these other styles, still within the framework of that tremendous classical discipline. In other words, over the years we've had the time to grow together, and our interactions and results keep getting stronger.

The same applies to the Orchestra. When we sat down with Alfred Brendel to work on the Beethoven concerti, I said to them, "Now look, you play the Beethoven concerti all the time. You've known the Beethoven concerti since before I was born. Some of you played it with Stock and Schnabel, for crying out loud! Okay—but now we want to try to

Chicago Symphony Chorus director Margaret Hillis works with James Levine during a 1984 rehearsal for *Carmina Burana*. The polish and skill of the Chorus make it possible to include important and seldom-performed choral works as a regular part of the Festival's repertoire.

144

Radivoj Lah, former performance coordinator and doublebassist of the CSO, reports to the music director at the start of a rehearsal in 1975.

James Levine at Ravinia in 1984.

Members of the Chicago Symphony warm up before a concert at Ravinia.

Chicago Symphony tuba player Arnold Jacobs, regarded by many of the world's most outstanding wind players as preeminent in his field.

James Levine shares the audience's warm welcome with Chicago Symphony co-concertmasters Samuel Magad (*left*) and Victor Aitay.

full-scale institute for students at Ravinia and introducing conceptually related artistic ideas that can't be explored in sufficient depth with only three or four weeks.

None of us thinks that outdoor concerts will replace indoor concerts or that records will replace live performances or that a concert opera performance will replace a fully staged opera. It just seems to me that one can argue all day about what the function of any arts organization is, and it seems to me that we solve the issue of Ravinia's specific identity very well. I look around at the beauty of the park, the acoustics and proportion of the Pavilion, the way we can use the Murray Theatre, the contributions of the artists-in-residence, and the Chicago Symphony Orchestra and Chorus in residence. Look how these people work during the Festival weeks—putting on performances of difficult music under extreme weather conditions sufficiently well to be worthy of recording, finishing one concert and getting up the next morning to rehearse for another. That quiet, lazy summer one reads about in novels is surely a remote romantic vision for the performers at Ravinia. But most of the people around Ravinia seem to find a rejuvenation synonymous with summer from the change of pace, the change of style, the challenge of new repertoire, and the opportunity to work from a different vantage point. It's that kind of thinking, that buoyant spirit, which has been prevalent throughout the unique history of Ravinia. And it's that spirit which makes Ravinia truly magical! [This piece derives from interviews with Maestro Levine.]

LOOKING TO THE FUTURE

Every generation of artists adds a generous measure of brilliance to the universe. Keeping that special brightness radiating throughout a world of rapid change and growing complexity calls for creative thinking about artistic directions and for goals that are more qualitative than quantitative.

I have long felt that many young artists never attain their potential as performers, not from any lack of fine teaching and necessary technical skills, but because they have not had certain opportunities at a critical time in their development. The most important opportunity of all is having a prominent performance platform, where listeners include peers, artistic leaders, and the important general public.

Ravinia traditionally has recognized its responsibility for creating performance opportunities for young artists at the start of their careers but only now, as the Festival enters its second half century, is Ravinia able to develop a comprehensive program of career-oriented training for exceptional young musicians, guaranteeing them a special performance at the Festival. This is the major thrust of Ravinia's long-desired Young Artists' Institute, which soon will become a reality.

The Institute will be housed in a splendid new building that will incorporate a 450-seat concert hall for performances as well as for master classes and other related functions. There will be administrative offices, teaching studios, practice rooms, and facilities for audio-visual taping and playback as a means of assisting both the young artist and the teacher in evaluating performances and stage presence.

Ravinia's management, trustees, and special committees concerned with the development of the plan have taken great care to insure that the design of the building is sympathetic with the character and openness of the park, yet distinct in style from existing buildings. The position of the new building, forming a triangular campus with the Pavilion and Murray Theatre, will open up prime lawn space for the Festival's growing audiences.

Initially, the program will focus on four instruments—piano, violin, viola, and cello—with instruction offered by Ravinia's visiting artist-teachers and a faculty of master teachers, including some members of the Chicago Symphony Orchestra. Other artistic expressions will be added as the program develops. Candidates for the Institute will be accepted into the program by audition.

The Institute has evolved from the summer series of master classes presented at the Festival since 1972 in collaboration with the Northwestern University School of Music. In this new venture, forty to fifty young artists will spend the summer studying and performing at Ravinia. The impact of the program, however, will go beyond the young artists; it will build an atmosphere that stimulates creativity through interaction among all members of the Ravinia musical community.

Imagine, if you will, James Levine stopping by the room where a group of student chamber musicians is struggling with a piece whose innate difficulties have produced musical frustrations that have gotten in the way of the enjoyment of the music. Imagine how much these young artists could learn from Levine about the work—and loving the process of discovery, loving performance, and lov-

156

An early rendering of the Young Artists' Institute, as planned by the Chicago architectural firm of Lubotsky, Metter, Worthington, and Law, Ltd.

ing music! And imagine how much Jim would enjoy seeing that moment of revelation in their eyes. This is the kind of expectation we want to fulfill through the Young Artists' Institute in the seasons ahead.

This unique program has the strong support of officials and residents in Highland Park where the Festival is situated. The City of Highland Park and the Ravinia Festival have developed a mutual pride in each other's accomplishments over the past fifty years. The artistic quality of the Festival and the beauty of the city are enjoyed annually by hundreds of thousands of visitors from near and far.

Always reaching for "the best of its kind" in any artistic idiom, Ravinia will continue to increase the scope and depth of its programs and provide the adventures its audiences expect. Sometimes these adventures mean taking risks, but in taking risks along the way Ravinia will continue its growth and the fulfillment of its artistic responsibilities in its second half century. Contemplating Ravinia's future can be as fascinating as remembering its past.

Edward Gordon

INDEX

PICTURE CREDITS